Cholesterol Rev____

Insider Secrets To Revitalising
Your Health And Lowering
Your Cholesterol Naturally!

- Stuart Brown -

Cholesterol is a silent killer, and you need to find out **NOW** how to combat it.

Cholesterol Revitaliser is a fast-track health solution that can help you to do exactly that.

It covers everything you need to know about effectively lowering your cholesterol.

It explores the information that you need to make informed, intelligent decisions about your health.

It discusses natural ways that you can dramatically lower your cholesterol, as well as the role that statins and supplements can play.

It outlines diet choices to lower cholesterol naturally and explores the amazing variety of foods that can re-invigorate your system.

Let *Cholesterol Revitaliser* be your guide on your journey to lower cholesterol and better health.

After you have read and enjoyed this book then please write a positive review on Amazon so that others can get to benefit as well.

You can find this book at the following web addresses on Amazon:

US - www.amazon.com/dp/0956436307
UK - www.amazon.co.uk/dp/0956436307
Canada - www.amazon.ca/dp/0956436307

Thanks.

Stuart Brown

About The Author:

Stuart Brown is passionate about health, vitality and being the best you can be. He believes that each of us has to do our part to ensure that we live the healthy lives we all deserve, and that great information is a fabulous starting point on that journey.

Cholesterol Revitaliser is his attempt to shed light on the subject of lowering your cholesterol in a way that is both effective and enjoyable.

Cholesterol Revitaliser

Insider Secrets To Revitalising Your Health And Lowering Your Cholesterol Naturally!

Stuart Brown

Revitaliser Publishing
Gidea Park, Essex

Health Disclaimer:

All material is provided for your information only and may not be construed as medical advice or instruction. You should visit your Doctor prior to any changes in diet, exercise or supplementation. No action or inaction should be taken based solely on the contents of this information; instead, readers should consult appropriate health professionals on any matter relating to their health and well-being.

The information and opinions expressed here are believed to be accurate, based on the best judgment of the author at the time of writing. Readers who fail to consult with appropriate health authorities assume the risk of any injuries. The author and publisher are not responsible for errors or omissions.

Contents

Introduction

We are about to embark on a journey together into the weird and wonderful world of your body and how you can start to lower your cholesterol levels in as little as thirty days.

If you are reading this, then the odds are that you are worried about cholesterol. And whether you are concerned because you have read statistics that suggest high cholesterol may be bad for you or because you, or someone you know has been diagnosed with having high levels of "bad" cholesterol, the fact is that we could all stand to learn more about this important health issue.

In fact, many health experts now think that high cholesterol levels are among the greatest health problems that face us today. In this guide, you will learn how to take control of your health.

What We Will Be Covering

In the next eight chapters we will be covering the following:

1/The Basics of Cholesterol
Understanding cholesterol, what cholesterol is and why it is Important.

2/Eating for Lower Cholesterol
The important role that diet can play in lowering your cholesterol and heart health in general.

3/The Cholesterol Conscious Chef - Cooking up a Storm (The Healthy Way!)

Important insights into the way you prepare and cook food that can affect your cholesterol.

4/Cholesterol Lowering Treatments, Drugs and How Changing Your Lifestyle Can Affect Your Cholesterol

From the many herbal remedies that can lower your cholesterol, to statin medications and exercise.

5/Dealing with Your Doctor and 8 Cholesterol Myths EXPLODED!

How to deal effectively with health care professionals, questions to ask and eight common cholesterol myths exploded.

6/Three Insider Cholesterol Secrets

How high cholesterol doesn't just affect adults. How to make your children (or grandchildren) "Food Smart". How advertising can affect your cholesterol and how you can turn "health food" into "convenience food".

7/The Cholesterol Conscious Chef Goes Shopping

How to shop more effectively to help achieve your goal of lowering your cholesterol.

8/Ten Cholesterol Goldmine Resources, 1 Must Have Item and The Cholesterol Revitaliser Power Summary

Where I wrap everything up into an easy summary and list resources where you can turn to for further help and information.

So that by the end of *Cholesterol Revitaliser,* you will know:

• What having cholesterol levels that are too high can do to you. And what treatments are available that can help you to lower your cholesterol.
• The exact steps you can take to live a heart healthy life.
• The Insider Secrets that can make healthy cholesterol levels achievable for you.
• How to speak to your doctor about cholesterol.
• The myths that can affect your health.
• And what to eat for a healthy heart.

You can use this book as you wish, read it all in one sitting or take it more slowly. I know there is a lot of information here. So it's entirely up to you.

Several things may contribute to high cholesterol, and several things can help lower it. And hence the steps that must be taken also vary with each person. This book does not dictate. It simply empowers you by giving you the tools you need to develop your own on-going program for a healthy cholesterol level. (And an all-round more vibrant you!)

Also, please be advised that while the advice and tips contained here can be very useful, if you feel that you may have high cholesterol, please consult a doctor. Your doctor can help you in devising a cholesterol lowering plan and can also help you determine which health tips may be most effective for your own particular situation.

So, let's get started towards lowering your cholesterol, a healthier heart and a more revitalised you!

Chapter 1
The Basics of Cholesterol

In order to understand why it's important to lower your cholesterol, it is necessary to first understand what cholesterol is. So let's get back to basics.

What Is Cholesterol?

Cholesterol is a fat-like waxy substance and is produced by the liver. Although some cholesterol is important to overall health and bodily functions, too much cholesterol in the body has damaging effects.

When the cholesterol level is appropriate, it plays a life-giving role in many functions of the body. When cholesterol is at a good level it works to build and repair cells, insulates nerve fibres (and hence allows nerve signals to travel properly) produces hormones such as oestrogen and testosterone, and other hormones which carry chemical signals around the body and produces bile acids which are proven to aid in the digestion of fat.

With too much cholesterol in the body though, the levels build up and cause damage by clogging your arteries. This puts you at serious risk for conditions such as heart attacks and strokes. In fact, the major cause behind heart attacks and strokes is clogged arteries resulting from high levels of cholesterol.

When you eat saturated foods such as dairy, meat and eggs your cholesterol elevates. On the other hand when you eat foods such as fruits, vegetables, and grains you can maintain optimal health as they are not from animal sources and hence don't contain cholesterol.

So, here is the first piece of really good news!

High cholesterol can generally be avoided! And the purpose of *Cholesterol Revitaliser* is to inform, educate and provide healthful options to make that happen.

With a nutritious diet, the 50% of adults with elevated cholesterol can regain their health and lower their risk of heart disease by 2% simply from reducing cholesterol by a mere 1%.

This is easily achievable.

Changes to your diet alone can reduce your cholesterol by between 10 to 15 per cent when you adopt heart healthy principles of eating fresh, low fat foods. With further reductions possible with proven herbal treatments such as Pantethine which has been shown to reduce total cholesterol and LDL Cholesterol by 10 to 15%, and also Niacin and others which I'll discuss much more in *Chapter 4 - Cholesterol Lowering Treatments*.

Plus the addition of Plant Sterols (which I'll discuss in *Chapter 7 - The Cholesterol Conscious Chef Goes Shopping*) into the diet can also reduce total cholesterol by 10 to 15%.

Then add in more exercise.

A recent study has shown that when you add in thirty minutes of exercise into your daily routine you can increase your Good HDL Cholesterol levels by over 5%. And the double whammy of exercising more and eating a healthier diet often has the effect of weight loss, which in turn leads to further reductions in LDL and Total Cholesterol.

There are lots of possibilities.

Cholesterol can be lowered in many different ways such as through diet, drugs and herbs, exercise and weight loss if you take an intelligent and considered approach to managing it.

And let me be clear. You should try out as many of the ideas as are applicable to you. Not just one or two. The best way to build a brick wall is to pile on the bricks. Not just lay one or two and then give up and go and eat a cheeseburger instead.

The same thing is true with lowering your cholesterol. If you exercise like mad and eat healthily for a week, but then give up and revert back to your previous ways of doing things, you aren't going to see any benefits.

This is a book. Not a magic wand ☺

The information in this book is about not only lowering your cholesterol, but also revitalising your health. And if that is going to happen, then simply eating a couple more carrots every week just isn't going to suffice.

As you progress with *Cholesterol Revitaliser* you will learn healthy, alternative ways to manage your cholesterol without having to rely on medications.

So, commit, here and now to being your best self. Not some pale imitation that you have gradually settled for.

The vibrant you is in there somewhere. And I am committed (with your help) to bringing it out permanently.

I do recommend that you visit your physician before making any changes, and also on a regular basis to keep a keen eye on your cholesterol levels and also general health. It is important to be safe.

I feel sure that if you step up here and commit to this program of positive changes that it will work out better than you ever dreamed possible.

Ok. So, let's first talk about **Understanding Cholesterol Levels.**

While most people talk about "cholesterol levels" there is in fact more than one type of cholesterol. In fact, there are several different body functions and several different substances that make up our understanding of "cholesterol."

As with some fats, cholesterol cannot be dissolved in the blood. Instead, molecules called lipoproteins carry it to and from cells. Molecules are made from an outer layer of protein and an inner core of both cholesterol and triglycerides, which is another form of fat.

Lipoproteins equip the cholesterol to move around the body.

The two main types of lipoproteins are:

1/ High Density Lipoproteins (HDL Cholesterol)

HDL transports cholesterol from cells back to the liver.

HDL is either reused or converts to bile acids and is then disposed of. You can think of this as *"good cholesterol"*. You want to ensure that your levels of HDL cholesterol remain high for optimum heart health, since having levels of HDL that are too low even when other cholesterol levels are normal, may lead to heart problems.

As you work to lower your "bad cholesterol" (more on that in a moment) it is important to also take steps to raise your HDL levels. HDL aids to ensure protection from the risk of heart attack and stroke. HDL consists of more protein than triglycerides or cholesterol, and helps to remove LDL from artery walls.

The second type of Lipoprotein is:

2/ Low Density Lipoproteins (LDL Cholesterol)

Low Density Lipoproteins carry approximately 60-70% of cholesterol around the body and can be thought of as *"bad cholesterol"*. Studies show conclusively that high LDL Cholesterol leads to much higher risk of heart attack and stroke. Other factors involved in this risk are age, gender, smoking, family history of heart disease, high blood pressure and having diabetes.

So, when we speak of "cholesterol levels" we mean more than one number. To maintain optimum health, you will need to know your levels of both LDL and HDL and will need to work hard to keep both levels in healthy ranges.

In order to gauge this effectively you should visit your Doctor to get your Cholesterol Levels tested.

Your Doctor will need to do a quick and painless blood test in order to facilitate this.

So, what constitutes a 'Good' Cholesterol Level?

Well, when your test report comes back from the Doctor it should show four different factors:

☐ Total Blood Cholesterol Level
☐ LDL (Bad Cholesterol) Level
☐ HDL (Good Cholesterol) Level
☐ Your Triglyceride Level

These will usually be reported in milligrams per deciliter of blood. You will commonly see this shortened to MG/DL.

Let's take a look at each of those in turn.

First, the **Total Blood Cholesterol Level**.
The American Heart Association has three distinct boundary levels for considering Total Blood Cholesterol Levels.

☐ Less than 200 milligrams per deciliter of blood is generally considered the desirable level.
☐ 200 to 239 milligrams per deciliter is a borderline high risk level.
☐ And over 240 milligrams per deciliter of blood you are generally considered to be high risk.

So what does that mean?

Well, if your total blood Cholesterol Level is less than 200 milligrams per deciliter of blood. And your HDL, LDL and Triglyceride levels (I'll discuss those later) are also at desirable levels, and you do not have any other risk factors counting against you such as smoking, family history of heart disease etc. Then you would generally be at a relatively low risk of coronary heart disease. So, your chances of being heart healthy are increased.

Now, if your reading does come back at less than 200 milligrams per deciliter of blood than that is great news. But don't get carried away. It's not a license to take up smoking, become a slob and start eating fatty foods! And you should still have it checked every few years to make sure you are still at healthy levels.

It can be very easy to loosen up and adopt lifestyle choices that don't serve our health well, and so even if you are currently at good levels it definitely pays dividends to be wary of becoming complacent about your health. You have precisely one body. And you need to make sure it stays in good shape.

If your total blood cholesterol level is between 200 and 239 milligrams per deciliter of blood, then this is generally considered a borderline risk level. What this means is that you need to work with your Doctor and get educated through books like this to make sure you are eating right, exercising and taking measures to make sure that you stay heart healthy.

It is possible to have borderline levels of total blood cholesterol (to remind you that's between 200 and 239 milligrams per deciliter of blood) and have normal levels of LDL Cholesterol (that's the bad guy). But have it balanced with high levels of HDL Cholesterol (that's the good guy). So it need not be bad news. But at this level you will need to be discussing options with your Doctor, and getting down to the detail of whether the reading is higher because of elevated readings of good or bad cholesterol, and the kind of life changes that you can take to normalize your levels.

Above 240 milligrams of cholesterol per deciliter of blood you are getting into the high risk category. This is bad news and you need to realize the dangers you are facing if you stay here. People who come into this high risk category (above 240 milligrams per deciliter of blood) have been shown to have twice the risk of coronary heart disease as those whose level is desirable (that's below 200). And it's urgent that you discuss your options with your Doctor, which may include medication.

You need to make sure that any test you get for Cholesterol shows the three different factors that are involved in Total Blood Cholesterol levels. Namely LDL (Bad) Cholesterol, HDL (Good) Cholesterol and Triglyceride levels. Because you really need to know each of these levels individually so that you can make an accurate assessment as to where you really stand with your cholesterol levels and any lifestyle changes you need to make.

Let's examine the **HDL or Good Cholesterol Readings.**

Here, contrary to what you might think, higher levels are actually better because having low HDL Cholesterol puts you at a higher risk for heart disease.

If we are looking at averages here, than a reading of less than 40 milligrams per deciliter of blood for men, and 50 milligrams per deciliter of blood for women would increase your chances of getting heart disease. A normal range would tend to be 40 to 50 for men and 50 to 60 for women, with the upper ranges in each case affording some protection against heart disease.

The good news is that in trying to Lower High Cholesterol you will most likely also raise your level of HDL or Good Cholesterol, because cutting out smoking, changing your diet and getting more exercise all help to raise your HDL levels.

Now let's take a look at what your **LDL or Bad Cholesterol Level** means.

The lower your LDL Cholesterol Levels are then correspondingly the lower are your risks of heart attacks and strokes. Your LDL Cholesterol level is a better gauge of your overall risk for heart problems than total blood cholesterol. So it is important to take a look at it.

If we are considering what levels are good and bad then the following are some good guidelines to keep in mind.

There are **five ranges that the _American Heart Association_ considers for LDL Cholesterol.** (**www.americanheart.org**)

☐ Less than 100 milligrams per decilitre of blood is considered optimal.
☐ 100 to 129 Milligrams is near optimal
☐ 130 to 159 milligrams is borderline high
☐ 160 to 189 milligrams is high
☐ And, above 190 milligrams per deciliter of blood is considered very high

What is important to consider with all these ranges is that they are good guidelines to bear in mind. But they are not set in stone. Everyone's physiology, history and genetics are different so a healthy level for you may be different from a healthy level for your friend or neighbour. But nevertheless, it is useful to know these broad figures because then it enables you to plan and research accordingly.

It is no good burying your head in the sand and kidding yourself that you don't have to take action if you have higher than optimal levels of LDL Cholesterol.

You Do. It's important.

It's YOUR health that is at stake, and whilst the first step on the road to fixing any problem is to identify it, if you then fail to do anything about it, the knowledge by itself will do nothing for you (except perhaps cause you sleepless nights). So, if in doubt get further tests carried out by your Doctor or health care practitioner. Then really drill down as to the details of your health profile, and what you need to do in order to get your cholesterol levels, and your health in general back on the right track.

The third component of the overall Blood Cholesterol Level is your **Triglyceride Level**.

Triglyceride is a form of fat and it tends to be the case that if you have high triglyceride levels then you will also have High LDL (Bad) Cholesterol, Low HDL (Good) Cholesterol and overall higher total blood cholesterol levels. The measurement levels for triglycerides can be considered within four bands.

☐ **Normal** or Optimal being less than 150 milligrams per deciliter of blood.

☐ **Borderline** High being 150 to 199 milligrams per deciliter of blood.

☐ **High** being 200 to 499 milligrams per deciliter, and...

☐ **Very High** being above 500 milligrams per deciliter of blood.

The typical causes of why you would have elevated levels of Triglycerides in your blood would be smoking, lack of exercise, high alcohol consumption and poor diet.

Fortunately, the good news is that in the process of lowering your Cholesterol back to optimal levels you can address each of those three.

Lifestyle factors are a big part of the things that you can actively control to get your health back on track. These include eating more healthily, making sure you don't overeat, cutting out smoking, and limiting your consumption of alcohol.

Understanding the Causes of High Cholesterol

Besides diet, other causes of high cholesterol are lifestyle, gender and the heritage of the individual.

For some people, even maintaining cholesterol at the right levels and being fit and thin will STILL not prevent the development of high levels of bad cholesterol. Due to heart risk factors besides diet, some people require a very aggressive approach which includes cholesterol lowering medication. (We will address these in Chapter 4 of Cholesterol Revitaliser – *"Cholesterol Lowering Treatments"*)

Different Lifestyle Issues

When we opt for convenience in eating over nutrition, we are setting ourselves up for problems. Eating fast foods and convenience foods results in eating too many fats and salts, which can raise our bad cholesterol levels (just to jog your memory that's the LDL Cholesterol).

In addition, a more sedentary lifestyle also contributes to unhealthy levels of cholesterol.

If you want to see a graphic representation of this, consider renting the documentary movie "*Supersize Me.*" This detailed how one man, Morgan Spurlock, changed his diet to only eat McDonalds fast foods and took no exercise for 30 days to see how it would affect his health. The results on his cholesterol and body health in just 30 days were truly frightening. After about 20 days his Doctor was advising him to stop because he feared there may be major long term health ramifications. And yet this was an average guy who until then had been a normal weight and was regularly exercising.

In the 30 day experiment he gained 24 pounds in weight and his cholesterol rose from a low level of 165 to a dangerously high 230 within the 30 days.

You can read about the results of his diet on Wikipedia here:

http://en.wikipedia.org/wiki/Super_Size_Me

That is the power that a change of diet can have.

The good news is that it can also happen in reverse. Lay off the junk food and get some exercise and you can start to repair any damage surprisingly quickly.

Practical Steps To Getting Started

Diet

An important consideration in eating is choosing lower fat food products.

Buy cooking oils that are unsaturated. Use low fat cooking sprays to replace heavy oils whenever possible. Reduce your overall use of oils even further by using cooking techniques that require little or no oil. Or at least choose healthier oils like Olive Oil.

A visit to a nutritionist or dietician could also be something you could explore to get further insights into your current eating habits.

Exercise

Regular exercise effectively lowers cholesterol and allows you to maintain your body strength and function at your best.

Just 20 minutes of aerobic exercise, including walking, each day will lower your cholesterol.

Exercise does not have to be a large time or financial commitment. Simple activities that get you moving and that you enjoy enough to repeat are almost always adequate.

Age and Gender

Oestrogen acts to raise HDL (Good) Cholesterol, so women also tend to have higher levels than men of HDL (Good) Cholesterol. This may help to explain why premenopausal women seem to have more protection against heart disease. They also tend to have higher triglyceride levels than men.

Cholesterol levels increase with age. While there is not much that you can do about your age, you can make sure that age does not threaten your heart health by sticking to a healthy lifestyle and diet and getting your cholesterol levels monitored regularly.

Heritage

Genetics play a key role in a person's health and this includes the amount of cholesterol you might have. One in 500 people has high cholesterol because of an inherited problem.

Find out if other members of your family battle with high levels of cholesterol and then bring this to your doctor's attention right away. If you have a family history of heart disease and high cholesterol levels, work harder and start earlier in adopting a healthy lifestyle and eating plan.

Your Arteries and Cholesterol

The job of your arteries is to pump blood. The Dorsal Aorta or the main artery, branches out into many smaller arteries. Each body system has arteries which are responsible for providing the oxygen rich blood that keeps us alive.

Too much cholesterol in the blood, especially LDL cholesterol, prevents arteries from working at their best. High levels of LDL cholesterol may even prevent arteries from functioning at all, since cholesterol can actually lead to blockages in your arteries. For this reason, it is critical that we keep arteries free of bad cholesterol to maintain optimal health.

Arteries are constructed of a tough exterior and a soft, smooth interior. Each artery has three specific layers:

• **The outer layer**
• **The middle (muscular) layer, and,**
• **The inner layer**

The middle layer is elastic and very strong. It helps pump the body's blood. The inner layer is smooth and allows the blood to flow easily. As the heart beats, the arteries expand and are filled with blood. The heart relaxes and produces enough force to push the blood through. In a healthy person, this system works effectively and the blood can carry oxygen and other essentials throughout the body.

Disease fills the arteries with fatty deposits and this becomes a dangerous obstacle to good health. High cholesterol levels fill arteries with thick substances that prevent your body from working well. Your heart becomes starved of required blood. If this happens often enough you can suffer a heart attack or a stroke.

WAKE UP CALL!

The main cause behind heart disease is this thickening of the fatty deposits in the arteries, and the main reason behind the blocking of arteries is high levels of LDL cholesterol. This means that if you want to prevent heart disease, heart attacks, and strokes, you need to keep your cholesterol levels in a healthy range.

Even having "borderline" cholesterol levels or levels that are elevated but not considered "very high" can increase your chances of heart disease or a stroke.

No matter what your current state of health, eating a better diet and getting adequate amounts of exercise can make you healthier.

The next chapter is coming up fast. But first, clear your mind and consider these sobering facts.

Heart disease is one of the leading killers in North America. In fact the *National Center for Health Statistics* (**www.cdc.gov/nchs/**) has estimated that 12% of adults in America are diagnosed with heart disease.

That is over 25 million people actually diagnosed by a health professional.

But in 2007 the *American Heart Association* (**www.americanheart.org**) estimated that even that figure is just the tip of the iceberg, and that an estimated 79,400,000 American Adults (1 in 3) have one or more types of cardiovascular disease.

In 2004 for example 871,517 people died of heart disease in America. In total this accounted for 36.3% of all 2,398,000 US Deaths in 2004, or 1 in every 2.8 deaths.

In fact, in every year since 1900, except 1918 (when there was a flu pandemic), cardiovascular disease has accounted for more deaths than any other single cause or group of causes of death in the United States.

According to the *American Heart Association*, over 105 million American Adults have total blood cholesterol levels above 200 milligrams per deciliter of blood, and 36.6 million people have levels above 240 milligrams per decilitre.

This means that about half the American population have borderline-high levels of cholesterol, and about 18% have high levels of cholesterol.

So this is a big problem.

And yet, lowering your cholesterol levels through a heart-healthy diet, nutrition and exercise regime is one of the best ways to prevent heart disease.

In the next chapter we will continue to explore how to make lower cholesterol a reality for you.

Chapter 2
Eating For Lower Cholesterol
The Important Role that Diet Can Play in Lowering Your Cholesterol and Heart Health In General

Eating is an important factor in good health that can affect your cholesterol level a great deal. If your cholesterol is too high, the foods you eat can be one of the things you can control most effectively to quickly lower your cholesterol. In fact, if you have elevated levels of cholesterol, a healthy diet is the one thing that you absolutely **MUST** do in order to ensure heart health.

Adapting to a Cholesterol Friendly Diet

Once your doctor has confirmed that you have high cholesterol, you can take steps to regain your health by following a low cholesterol and low fat diet.

Being true to such a healthy diet will ensure that you can reduce total cholesterol levels by as much as 15 per cent. As an added benefit, this sort of diet will also make you feel generally healthier and more energetic as well.

You would also benefit further from starting a regular exercise schedule which helps to raise your "good" HDL cholesterol levels for a total package of healthy living. Plus exercising has many benefits beyond just reducing your LDL Cholesterol and raising your HDL Cholesterol.

Christine Albert and *William Whang* followed the activities of 85,000 women for 24 years in a study at Harvard.

In 2006 *William Whang* concluded:

"The women who reported exercising four or more hours a week had a 59 per cent lower risk of sudden cardiac death over 18 years of follow up compared to women who reported not exercising at all".

And similar effects have been reported with men.

So starting up a regular exercise regime is a great way to get your health back on track. Especially when you consider the fact that Cardiovascular Disease accounts for 1 in 3 deaths in America and the UK.

So, combine a healthy diet with exercise. And within as short a time as 30 days you will start to experience a renewed sense of energy and vitality. And longer term the effects in your overall health can be incredible.

Following a low cholesterol and low fat diet necessitates that you must do the following:

• Get less than 7% of your day's total calories from saturated fat. In fact, try to lower your saturated fat intake as far as possible. Your doctor may even recommend that you get a smaller percentage of your calories from saturated fat, especially if you have very high cholesterol.

• Receive 25-35% or less of your day's total calories from fat. Again, your doctor may recommend that you consume an even smaller amount of fat than this.

• Ideally consume less than 200 milligrams of dietary cholesterol each day, or follow the limits for dietary cholesterol that your doctor sets for you. (The American Heart Association recommends that you limit your average daily cholesterol intake to less than 300 milligrams. If you have heart disease, they recommend limiting your daily intake to less than 200 milligrams.)

Cut Down On The Salt

Limit your sodium intake to less than 2400 milligrams a day. This is equivalent to less than one teaspoon a day.

The main source of sodium in our diets is salt. Salt is 40% sodium and 60% chloride. So, overall that means 2 and a half teaspoons of salt would be roughly 2400 milligrams of sodium.

Note though, that this desired figure includes all the 'hidden' salt in processed foods which often accounts for as much as 80% of your daily intake of salt. So you need to start reading food labels as well as applying less salt to your meals directly.

Two studies reported in the April 19th 2007 issue of the *British Medical Journal* showed that people who cut back on the amount of salt in their diets by 25 to 35 per cent could reduce their risk of cardiovascular disease by as much as 25 per cent and lower their mortality rates by 20 per cent.

To give you some idea of how much salt there really is in the food we eat, here are some figures:

☐ Two large scrambled eggs have 342 milligrams of salt.
☐ One slice of luncheon meat has 350 milligrams of salt.
☐ Half a cup of canned green beans has 177 milligrams of salt.

So, it is easy to see how it can quickly add up in your diet, even if you don't hit the salt shaker.

Forewarned is forearmed though. So get into the habit of reading food labels and finding out how much salt is contained in the foods you regularly eat. It could be that there are low salt alternatives that taste virtually the same, or you could choose to cut down or eliminate certain high salt foods from your diet.

It doesn't have to only be about cutting down or eliminating foods though. Fresh vegetables and fruit taste great and are naturally low in salt. So eat more of those.

You should be resolved to eat only enough calories to improve your healthy weight and reduce your blood cholesterol level.

You Might Even Increase Your Lifespan

In fact, science is starting to reveal a direct link between cutting the amount of calories we eat (whilst still eating vital nutrients) and lifespan in general (Caveat here - In worms and monkeys! Bear with me).

The *BBC* reported in May 2007 on a nematode worm study published in the magazine *Nature* that found a Gene called the PHA4 gene that produced longer living worms, when they consumed less calories.

Now, let me be clear. This was not a human study. Humans are not worms. So it's not clear whether this is applicable to humans. But it is interesting. The amount of calories the worms ate directly affected their lifespan.

And more recent research in July 2009 on Rhesus Macaque Monkeys came to much the same conclusion after researchers from the University of Wisconsin-Madison reported the findings of a 20 year study. Professor Richard Weindruch who was involved in the study was reported as saying:

"We observed that caloric restriction reduced the risk of developing an age-related disease by a factor of three and increased survival."

(You can read more about the study here - **www.sciencemag.org/cgi/content/abstract/325/5937/201**)

What is clear is that being overweight can contribute to higher cholesterol and to heart ailments. So make sure that your diet supports your health rather than harms it, as it is important from many different perspectives.

Dieticians

If you want tailored assistance, seek out a nutritionist or dietician who can help you to devise an eating plan that you will stick to and enjoy.

In the United States you can find details of a dietician in your area from the *American Dietetic Association.*

www.eatright.org/Public/

In the United Kingdom you can find the same information from the *British Dietetic Association.*

www.bda.uk.com

You should not think about food in terms of dieting. You should think about which food empowers you to be your best, fittest, most healthy self.

You wouldn't put cooking oil in your car. It's the wrong fuel. So don't make the same mistake with your body. Only eat food that revitalises you.

Let's start looking at what that means.

Firstly, refuse foods made with harmful trans fats and saturated fats such as margarine, salad dressing and sauces.

The reason that you should refuse foods with Trans Fats particularly is because it is becoming increasingly clear that all fats are not created equal.

The Four Types of Dietary Fats

The four different types of dietary fats are Mono-unsaturated, Polyunsaturated, Saturated and Trans Fats, and each plays a critical role with your cholesterol levels.

Firstly, remember the two main types of cholesterol I spoke about earlier. LDL Cholesterol or 'Bad' Cholesterol and HDL or 'Good' Cholesterol. We want to raise our HDL Cholesterol and Lower our LDL Cholesterol.

Let's now look at those four dietary fats and drill down.

1/ Monounsaturated Fat

Good sources for monounsaturated fat are olives, peanut oil, almonds, cashews, canola oil and avocadoes.

The effect that this has on your Cholesterol Levels is to Lower LDL Cholesterol and Raise HDL Cholesterol.

The Bottom Line –
Monounsaturated Fat = A Goody.

2/ Saturated Fat

Sources for saturated dietary fats include cheese, red meat, chocolate, coconut milk, butter, coconut oil and milk. The effect that this has on your Cholesterol Levels is to raise both LDL Cholesterol and also raise HDL Levels. So in a way it is like giving with one hand, but taking with the other. Raising the LDL levels being bad, but raising the HDL Levels being good.

The Bottom Line – In general best avoided. But certainly lower your intake of saturated fats.

3/ Polyunsaturated Fat

Good sources for polyunsaturated fats include corn, soybean, cotton seed oils, fish and safflower.

The effect that this has on your cholesterol levels is to Lower LDL Cholesterol and Raise HDL Cholesterol.

The Bottom Line –
Polyunsaturated Fat = A Goody.

4/ Trans Fats

Sources for trans fats in the diet include vegetable shortening, partially hydrogenated vegetable oil, most margarines, deep fried chips, many fast foods, and many baked goods.

The effect that this has on your cholesterol levels is to Raise LDL Cholesterol, and decrease HDL Cholesterol.

The Bottom Line – Avoid at all costs.
Trans Fats = The Worst Baddy.

So, the message here is that you really need to look closely at those food labels and pay close attention to what you are eating. (Read Appendix 3 - "Learn To Read Food Labels").

The reality is that most on the shelf products in the grocery store have a mix of these fats. And so it can seem quite confusing. But you really just need to remember it like this.

The Best Fats are monounsaturated and polyunsaturated. Eat more of these as the science supports the conclusion that it actually lowers your risk of heart disease.

In the Harvard Nurses Study that I have spoken about previously, the researchers found that replacing 80 calories of carbohydrates with 80 calories of either polyunsaturated or monounsaturated fat lowered the risk of heart disease by 30 to 40 per cent.

Saturated Fats are a different matter entirely. You certainly should reduce your intake of saturated fat wherever possible. Because it does raise your LDL (Bad) Cholesterol, and increase your risks of heart disease. But as a part of a balanced diet there is no problem with having eggs or cheese for example. You just need to do it in moderation.

Far worse than saturated fats are trans fats. You should actively avoid these.

Trans Fats are commonly used to prolong the shelf life of foods. They also have a higher melting point so are attractive for baking. So, be sure to check those food labels and avoid foods with trans fats.

In the Harvard Nurses study they found that when they replaced only 30 calories (equivalent to 7 grams) of carbohydrates every day with 30 calories (equivalent to 4 grams) of trans fats. That it nearly doubled the risk for heart disease. So this is very bad news for your health.

Think about that in a different way. The next time you go out food shopping take a look at a candy bar. Look at how many grams it weighs. Many chocolate bars for example are 100 grams. Then try to picture in your mind how little 4 grams really is.

In size terms it might be the equivalent of one twentieth the size of a chocolate bar.

In fact, here's another example. A packet of Maltesers weighs 58.5 grams. I counted out the Maltesers in a pack and there were 29. So one Malteser weighs roughly 2 grams. In other words 4 grams is the equivalent weight wise of just 2 Maltesers! (Though the Maltesers themselves actually tasted pretty good ☺)

It is staggeringly small. And yet just adding that small amount of trans fat to your diet on a daily basis has massively bad consequences for your health.

It's worth repeating.

Almost double the risk of heart disease. So really wake up to the risks.

Steer clear of shortening and many margarines as they have considerable amounts of trans fats.

Enjoy foods high in soluble fibre. These foods include:

• Oats, rye, and barley
• Fruits (especially try oranges and pears)
• Vegetables (especially brussel sprouts and carrots)
• Dried peas and beans

Avoid the following foods for best health:

• High cholesterol foods can increase your level of blood cholesterol. High cholesterol foods include:
• Organ meats (this includes liver, which may be eaten in small quantities)
• Egg yolks
• Full fat dairy products

Fried and processed foods are often high in fat and salt, which can wreak havoc on your heart health.

Limit and eat only in moderation if at all:

• Highly processed foods, and especially processed meats such as deli meats, sausages, hot dogs, salami and fatty red meats.
• All foods that are fried, especially deep fried foods.

You will produce meals that have lower saturated fats when you try the following methods of food preparation:

• Baking
• Broiling
• Microwaving
• Poaching
• Steaming
• Grilling
• Roasting (But only if you remove fats that are melted in the process)

Also, lightly stir-frying or sautéing using low-fat and low-salt broth is a good strategy.

Selecting your Foods

Enjoy a wide variety of foods regularly, including select cuts of meat, poultry, fish, dry beans, eggs and nuts each week.
    You can also keep your blood cholesterol levels low by doing the following:

• Choose chicken and turkey that has the skin removed. You can keep the skin on to seal in the juices so long as you remove the skin before eating.
• When selecting meat, choose leaner cuts, white meat, and cuts that have less white "marbleized" texture. The white "marble" is fat that can increase your cholesterol.
• Select fish such as cod that has less saturated fat than even chicken or other meats..
• Even the leanest cuts of meat, chicken and fish, have saturated fat and cholesterol so limit your daily intake to 6 ounces or

less (That's equivalent in size to about 2 packs of playing cards).

• You can increase soluble fibre intake if LDL is not lowered enough from reducing saturated fat and cholesterol rich foods.

One of the best things you can do for your cholesterol levels is to eat more fresh fruits and vegetables. Not only do these foods have no dietary cholesterol that can raise your bad cholesterol levels, but eating more fruits and vegetables has been linked to lowering cholesterol and risk of heart problems in patients.

Research studies have proven numerous times that one of the best things you can do for yourself if you are worried about your cholesterol level is to eat more fresh fruit and vegetables.

And the relationship to heart health is backed up conclusively by scientific studies.

The Harvard University based *"Nurses Health Study"'* and *"Health Professionals Follow Up Study"* included almost 110,000 people in it whose diet and health were monitored over the course of 14 years. These studies found a direct correlation between the amount of fruit and vegetables eaten and a person's risk of developing cardiovascular disease.

The group who averaged 8 or more servings of fruit and vegetables a day were 30% less likely to have a heart attack or stroke then the group who averaged less than one and a half servings of fruit and vegetables a day.

And it's not just "big" fruit and vegetable eaters (the eight portions a day group) who can benefit from changing their approach to food. In the two Harvard Studies they found that for every extra serving of fruits and vegetables a day that the participants added to their diets, their risk of heart disease **dropped by 4 per cent**.

Even modifying your diet a little then and adding in a couple of extra fruits or vegetables can dramatically lessen your chances of heart problems.

As an added bonus it can also have a favourable impact on lowering your blood pressure, which is another primary cause of strokes and heart attacks.

In *"The National Heart, Lung and Blood Institute Family Heart Study"* in 2004 it was shown that on average the 4466 people involved in the study consumed just over 3 servings of fruit and vegetables each day. But that of that group, those who consumed the most fruit and vegetables, on average over 4 servings a day, had significantly lower levels of LDL Cholesterol than those with lower consumptions.

Studies show that North Americans eat far less fresh fruits and vegetables than they should eat. A fact that has often been suggested as a key cause of the high cholesterol and heart disease levels in the United States. Not to mention the higher rates of obesity from which many North Americans suffer.

To put it simply, those nations that eat more fruits, vegetables, and grains are healthier and have lower cholesterol levels as a whole.

As an added bonus, you do not have to worry as much about eating too many fruits and vegetables. They are good for you and generally have fewer calories.

Whilst you do not want to overeat, you can eat far more fresh produce than meat products or chocolate cake and remain heart healthy. You can only eat small portions of animal products before you have to consider cholesterol content.

With vegetables and fruits, there is no such concern. If you have always felt deprived while following low-fat diets in the past, you can avoid this in the future simply by eating more of the "fresh stuff" and stop counting calories.

Key Point - Increasing your intake of fresh fruits and vegetables significantly should be your first goal as you try to lower your cholesterol over the next 30 days.

Remember that statistic from the Harvard Study. A 4% reduction in heart disease for each extra piece of fruit or vegetable you eat on a daily basis. If you could increase your salary by 4% just by eating an extra carrot a day would you do it? Sure you would. So give your body a gift and do the same for your health.

The Fruit and Vegetable Mission

One of the easiest ways to introduce these into the diet is to actively set out to buy new types of food when you go out shopping.

When most of us think of "veggies" we think only of a few, and we aren't necessarily doing cartwheels at the thought of eating them.

Much of this ambivalence has to do with the fact that we are not very adventurous in our choices.

In fact, there are many types of delicious fresh produce out there that can create spectacular meals while helping you to lower your cholesterol.

Consider all the vegetables you may not have tried yet.

I have given you a massive list of *"Fabulous Fruit and Vegetables"* in the appendix at the back of this book. That list represents just a small taster of all the delicious new foods that you may have been missing out on up until now. But at least serves to illustrate that there are many more vegetables then cabbage, potatoes and sprouts, and many more fruits then apples, oranges and bananas.

So check them out and think about trying something new the next time you visit the grocery store.

Here's a suggestion.

How about picking out a new fruit or vegetable to try each week? (Making it a "Mission" gives it extra priority)

Doing this will have several effects:

1/ It will not only help lower your cholesterol, but will also spice up your diet and keep it varied. Variety is the spice of life, and you should always be trying out new things.

2/ Shopping becomes more fun!

3/ It serves to illustrate that whilst the types of meats most people eat are really very limited. That the variety of fruit and vegetables is fantastically varied. It's just that most of us don't avail ourselves of that choice.

It would be normal to get bored of eating the same thing every day.

So mix it up and try something new.

Take a chance today and pick up something that you have never tried before. Your taste buds and your cholesterol level will thank you for it.

Make it a mission to find new and exciting foods on a regular basis that you can enjoy fresh to revitalise your health.

The secret to healthy eating is to make eating the right foods as attractive as eating the wrong foods. When you have many types of healthy and delicious foods to choose from, you will naturally choose foods that are good for you and for your heart. Introducing variety into your diet is one sure way to do this.

Over the next 30 days, use those two lists of fruits and vegetables, in the appendix at the back of this book, as a starting point for your adventures (Or simply pick something new to try whenever you go grocery shopping).

How do you climb a mountain?
One step at a time.
How do you lower your cholesterol?
One bite at a time.

Remember, from small acorns do mighty oak trees grow. So don't underestimate the power of just getting started in a small way.

One new "taste adventure" a week is better than doing nothing. And you can always build momentum over time.

So relax and have fun with it. Lowering your Cholesterol and improving your diet should be fun!

The more you throw yourself into making positive changes the more change you will experience for the better.

Chapter 3
The Cholesterol Conscious Chef
Cooking up a Storm
(The Healthy Way!)

If you want to lower your cholesterol, you will want to cook your own meals more often. This is firstly because many restaurants add lots of fat and salt to their foods in order to cheaply add texture and taste. And secondly because you really want to have maximum control over exactly what you put in your body.

Tips on How To Prepare Food

Convenience foods, are notorious for offering poor nutrition and plenty of fat, salt, and sugar.
So if you want to lower your cholesterol, then avoiding all fast-food, convenience, and pre-packaged meals is a great step to take.

Buy some fresh herbs. Use these to add flavour to your cooking rather than relying on salt.

If you have recipes you cannot part with, switch ingredients to healthier alternatives. Use good olive oil instead of butter, low-fat products instead of the regular kind and experiment with cutting salt out of recipes entirely.

This isn't hard to do, even if you are lost in the kitchen. There are a number of very fast and easy ways to ensure that you can whip up tasty and cholesterol-friendly meals no matter how harried your schedule.

If you are very busy and tired at the end of a long day, a salad and sandwich take less time to put together than it takes to phone the pizza parlour and get it delivered.

Wrap some veggies in a tortilla, cut more veggies into a salad, and drizzle the salad with olive oil and lemon juice. Use a mashed avocado or salt-free salsa as the "dressing" on your sandwich.

Soups and stir-fries are other kitchen friends of busy people who aren't very handy in the kitchen.

Keep fresh ingredients on hand and don't tempt yourself by keeping convenience foods and junk food in your house.

Choose fresh ingredients, the very freshest you can find. Not only is this healthier for you, but you will need less fat and salt in your cooking if your food ingredients are flavourful on their own.

Find low-fat and cholesterol-friendly recipes in cookbooks and plan to make these recipes. There are many recipe books available at your local library that feature heart-healthy and fast recipes that can make cholesterol-friendly eating a snap. And a search on Google for *"low cholesterol recipes"* yields more recipes then you could possibly make in an entire lifetime!

Don't overlook cookbooks that feature Chinese, Japanese, Raw food, Vegan, and Indian recipes. These are often heart-friendly and contain enough variety to keep you happy with your diet forever.

Cooking to lower your cholesterol is not very hard. There are a few basic foods that almost anyone can make that can keep your health in good shape.

Salads

Even if you are not an excellent cook, you can easily create a salad that is enticing. Simply chop up some favourite salad greens (cucumbers, tomatoes, carrots, zucchini, herbs) and garnish with a few nuts.

You can make your own dressing by mixing herbs (such as basil or thyme) and a squirt of lemon or you can choose prepared dressings that are very low in salt and fats.

You can also create a very low fat salad dressing by combining half an avocado with some herbs and lemon juice.

Avoid croutons, bacon bits, whole milk products such as chesses, eggs, and other high-fat foods in your salads.

If you do want to add meat to your salad, opt for skinless poultry.

Fruit Salads

Chopping up some of your favourite fruits, berries, and lemons can make a beautiful and attractive salad that is very low in fat.

If you are using apples or other fruits that tend to "brown" in your salad, a squirt of lemon juice over your salad will keep your fruit salad attractive and healthy.

A fruit salad is a great choice for breakfast or a later meal. It is appropriate even for those who have very high cholesterol and so must follow a more restrictive diet.

Sandwiches

Sandwiches are easy to make. Simply choose healthy breads, pitas or tortillas that are low in fats and salts and choose lots of vegetables for your sandwiches.

Avoid highly processed deli and sandwich meats. Instead, use lean and skinless chicken or other poultry.

Instead of fats or mayonnaise on your sandwiches (which can increase the fat content of your sandwiches considerably) choose to flavour your sandwich with fresh sweet onions or low-sodium mustard or salsa.

Pastas

There are a number of pastas available, from fresh pasta or dried pasta to vegetable pastas and rice pastas. All of these can be made into delicious and heart-friendly meals in minutes.

Simply cook the pasta in a pot. Shred your favourite vegetables or cut them into very small pieces. Combine the vegetables with some low-sodium and low-fat chicken or vegetable broth and cook until vegetables are softer but still crisp.

Add the pasta and toss until the vegetables are the desired consistency.

Add your favourite fresh herbs (basil is a good choice) and combine. This can be a very tasty combination and is still quite healthy for you. You can make similar meals with rice or even low-fat tofu.

Many prepared pasta dishes use plenty of salt or cream-based sauces, but some combination of this recipe can give you a tasty meal with less fat.

Smoothies

Combine your favourite fresh fruits in a blender with fresh fruit juice and a small squirt of honey.

Combine until blended.

This makes an excellent and very healthy snack. It can also be a great quick breakfast on days when you are in a rush.

Experiment with different fruit combinations to find different tastes.

Chilling or even freezing some of the fruit before serving can produce a nice chilled drink that is perfect for summer.

If you are craving desserts, you can add a small amount of very low fat frozen yogurt to this recipe and use frozen fruits to get a tasty and heart-friendly alternative to ice cream and other desserts.

Grilled Dishes

Brushing vegetables and lean meats with lemon juice and herbs and grilling on the barbeque is a great way to enjoy fat-free good-for-you foods that are easy and fast to create.

Lean Meat Dishes

When you have chosen your lean cuts of meat, you can make these foods even healthier by reducing the amount of fat you use in preparing them.

For example, marinating poultry and other meats in lemon juice and fresh dill or in pureed fruits and vegetables is a heart-friendly way to get plenty of flavours into your cooking without adding fat.

At many fish shops, you can get planks of cedar that are perfect for baking or grilling fish. Simply place the fish on the cedar, cover with lemon juice and possibly herbs and grill or bake until done.

Desserts and Snacks

Limiting desserts and snacks in general can help you control your weight and your calorie intake and so keep your heart healthy.

If you absolutely crave a dessert or snack, though, try to stave off the craving with fresh fruit.

If this does not work, then you can occasionally eat low-fat desserts and snacks such as angel food cake, fig and fruit bars. Low-fat yogurt, fruit sherbet, animal or graham crackers, wafers, and puddings made with low-fat milk can also make good lower-fat alternatives.

However, these products still do often contain salt, plenty of calories and some fats, so avoid overindulging and take care to read the labels on these snacks and choose the brands with the least sugar, calories, fat, and salt that you can.

Ok. So let's review what Eating for Lower Cholesterol really entails.

A low cholesterol, healthy diet is achieved by eating foods low in saturated fat and trans fats and concentrating on the following:

•Use herbs instead of salt in cooking.
•Consume fat free, skimmed, or 1% dairy products.
•Watch out for bottled and canned drinks and especially sports beverages. Many are very high in sodium, calories, and sugars.
•Choose only lean meats. Enjoy white meats, fish, and poultry rather than red meats.
•Eat plenty of fish and enjoy only skinless poultry.
•Select plenty of whole grain foods.
•Choose fresh rather than processed, spiced, prepared, pickled or tinned foods.
•If you cannot find fresh produce out of season, try frozen foods that have no sauces or other ingredients added.
•Eat lots of vegetables and fruit.
•Read food labels and choose foods that are low in fats (especially saturated and trans fats), sodium and cholesterol.

Chapter 4
Cholesterol-Lowering Treatments, Drugs and How Changing Your Lifestyle Can Affect Your Cholesterol

If your doctor has determined that you have heightened levels of LDL cholesterol, he or she will likely make some suggestions about things you may do in order to improve your health. Some of these suggestions will have to do with diet and lifestyle changes. However, if your cholesterol is quite high or you require an aggressive approach to lowering cholesterol, you may be advised to take certain medications or treatments in order to lower your cholesterol.

It is important that you know about the treatments and remedies that are available to lower cholesterol, as this will help you to work with your health practitioner to develop a cholesterol treatment regime that can work for you.

Healthy Cholesterol through Herbal and Natural Remedies

Scientific research is providing good evidence that there are several effective natural herbal remedies and supplements that help to lower LDL "bad" and raise HDL or "good" cholesterol.

If you visit a naturopath or health care practitioner who specializes in alternative medicines, you may be advised to try some of these treatments.

You can find a Naturopath in the US here:

www.naturopathic.org

And here in the UK:

www.naturopathy.org.uk

If you are worried about the side effects of pharmaceutical cholesterol-lowering drugs or treatments, you can speak with your
doctor about drug-free ways to lower cholesterol.

Considering alternative remedies gives those dealing
with higher levels of cholesterol new options. It is especially
good for those who do not react well to traditional pharmaceutical cholesterol-lowering medications.

Here are some alternative's to statins that you can discuss with your Doctor.

Guggul

Guggul gum resin from the mukul myrrh tree is used to treat
obesity. This same remedy is used to help lower cholesterol and
decrease blood pressure. Guggul is also named Guggulipid and
Gum guggulu. The botanical name is Commiphora mukul.
Guggul has been used to lower elevated cholesterol and triglycerides.

The active ingredients are resin, volatile oils, and gum.

There have been many clinical studies that highlight that
Guggul Therapy can lower LDL Cholesterol levels and triglyceride levels, some of which showed it lowering LDL Cholesterol
levels by over 10%.

However, this should be treated with caution, as a 2003
study published in *The Journal of the American Medical Association* found no benefit to taking the extract in a test group of
103 Americans. And in fact noted a moderate rise in LDL Cholesterol levels of participants.

This serves to highlight one of the big problems with many medical studies. Namely that they often contradict one another.

It may however be worth discussing this particular remedy with your Doctor, and getting their opinion. As the 2003 study does somewhat stand out as being the exception to other previous clinical studies that showed Guggul as being an effective treatment for lowering cholesterol.

However, please note that other herbal treatments such as Niacin and Pantethine (which I'll discuss shortly) have more consistent track records in clinical trials and so may be worth trying first.

Policosanol

This comes from sugar cane wax, and is another case in point of seemingly conflicting research results.

It has been touted as a safe and effective treatment to lower LDL cholesterol. With previous research saying that it promotes normal blood flow and lowers LDL Cholesterol.

However, research by German scientists from the *Medical Association* in Berlin in the May 2007 edition of *The Journal of the American Medical Association* conflicts with this.

They carried out trials on 143 Caucasian Adults with LDL Cholesterol levels of at least 150 milligrams per decilitre of blood. The participants of the study were randomly assigned to take Policosanol at 10, 20, 40 or 80 milligrams daily or a placebo. And were monitored for 12 weeks.

The study found no clinically significant effect on LDL Cholesterol, HDL Cholesterol or Triglycerides in any of the groups. Dr Heiner Berthold from the study noted that whilst the safety profile (the lack of side effects from taking Policosanol) was excellent. That almost all previous studies into Policosanol were published by one group in Cuba, whose research was funded by Dalmar Laboratories, which markets Policosanol.

He concluded that *"more independent studies are required to counterbalance the vast body of available positive trials"*.

Ok. Onto the treatments that have clearer science to back up their effectiveness.

Pantethine

Pantethine is a very promising cholesterol-lowering substance. It is a derivative of Vitamin B5, pantothenic acid. And has significantly reduced serum triglycerides, total cholesterol, and LDL Cholesterol or "bad cholesterol" levels. While increasing HDL or "good cholesterol" levels in several clinical trials.

In 2005 the Journal *"Nutrition Research"* undertook an analysis of 28 different human research studies into Pantethine between 1966 and 2002 that explored its relationship to lowering Cholesterol levels.

Looking at the results overall they found that by taking a dose of 900 mg of Pantethine daily, the subjects of the trials on average reduced their total cholesterol levels by an average of 8.7% by the end of month one.

Additionally they found that with each passing month of taking Pantethine that the results improved, until by month four the subjects had reduced their total cholesterol levels by an average of 15%.

Looking beyond those raw total cholesterol figures to a breakdown of the individual levels for LDL Cholesterol, HDL Cholesterol and Triglycerides the results were even more impressive.

The study found that over a four month period. The LDL Cholesterol levels dropped 10 to 20%. The Triglyceride Levels dropped by 14 to 33%. While Good HDL Cholesterol increased by about 10% over the period.

And remember this was simply by taking a 900mg daily supplement of Pantethine for 4 months.

The other good news is that Pantethine is actually very well tolerated by the body, and doesn't suffer with the many unfortunate side effects that commercial drug treatments of high cholesterol sometimes do. It also has a beneficial effect on raising HDL Cholesterol levels.

Do bear in mind that the effects are cumulative, so you will have to take it for the 4 month period mentioned by *Nutrition Research* in order to get the full benefits.

As with all other treatments here, you should consult your Doctor before starting a program of treatment.

Niacin

Nicotinic acid or Vitamin B3 is also called niacin, and is an important B Vitamin which is available cheaply and easily over the counter. It is perhaps the most effective treatment currently available for raising 'Good' HDL Cholesterol Levels. With high doses of it being able to raise HDL Levels by between 15 to 35%.

However, patients who take this medication need to have careful doctor supervision, since Niacin can have a number of side effects. By far the most common being hot flushes (which though annoying are generally not harmful).

Other potential side effects are however more serious, such as interactions with high blood pressure medicine, nausea, diarrhoea, vomiting, indigestion, gas, liver problems, gout, and high blood sugar.

If you have other medical conditions your doctor may decide that it is too risky because of these possible side effects.

However, Niacin is so effective at raising HDL Cholesterol levels, at high doses, that it is one of the few 'natural therapies' to have had considerable research fire-power dedicated to cracking its secrets and is widely used in treating high cholesterol.

Dr Martin Thoenes of the *Technical University*, Dresden, Germany reported the results of one such study at the 2007 *American College of Cardiology* Annual Scientific Session meeting in New Orleans. Where he had 50 test subjects over the age of 18 who were unable or unwilling to take a statin treatment.

After 52 weeks, compared with the placebo group, treatment with 1 gram daily of ER Niacin (a form of slow release Niacin) led to a 17% decrease in LDL Cholesterol, a significant decrease in Triglycerides and a significant 24% increase in HDL Cholesterol.

Three of the fifty participants dropped out before the end because of severe hot flushes.

However, hot flushes in general from taking Niacin are more common in other studies, (even if the participants didn't drop out). Where hot flushes are reported at different times in over 50% of people taking Niacin in high doses. (Though, as I have said, in most cases, the hot flushes are not significant enough to stop the participants from continuing)

In many cases, patients are started on small doses of Niacin and have their dosage slowly raised to an average daily dose of 1.5 to 3 grams per day to heighten the cholesterol-fighting power of this medication. It is found in two different types. Immediate release and timed release, and you will have to discuss with your Doctor which type is best for you.

Niacin can be taken with meals to reduce side effects such as hot flushes, and some doctors even suggest that patients combine it with taking aspirin as aspirin can help to counteract this flushing effect.

Also, bear in mind that because of the effect that Niacin has on blood sugar your Doctor is unlikely to prescribe it if you are a diabetic. Additionally, if you suffer from high blood pressure, then that would also need to be monitored closely whilst taking Niacin.

If you do fit a profile though that can tolerate it (which your Doctor can advise) then you could find it a very effective treatment as it can reduce LDL Cholesterol by 10 to 20 per cent. Reduce Triglycerides by 20 to 50 per cent and of vital consideration is its ability to raise HDL Cholesterol by 15 to 35 per cent.

Garlic

Garlic is a herb that has long been renowned for its benefits to heart health. As well as being a very popular dietary supplement, it is also commonly used to flavour food. Per capita consumption of Garlic was 2.6 pounds in 2004 in the US, with the United States being the world's largest importer of Garlic and China accounting for 75% of the world's supply.

A *National Institute of Health* Funded clinical trial published on the 26th February 2007 by the *Archives of Internal Medicine* has however cast doubt as to the cholesterol lowering properties of Garlic which have previously been touted in many studies.

The study was carried out over a period of 6 months and involved 192 individuals with elevated LDL Cholesterol ranging from 130 to 190 milligrams per decilitre of blood.

These individuals were then provided with sandwiches and tablets daily which contained one of four treatments. Raw Garlic, powdered garlic supplements, aged garlic extract supplements or a placebo.

Unfortunately, after 6 months the study found no evidence that either fresh garlic or garlic supplements were able to reduce cholesterol levels.

This flies in the face of previous studies that have shown Garlic as having an effect on lowering cholesterol. With even the lead author of the study *Dr Christopher Gardner* noting the fact that five previous meta analyses over the last few decades i.e. where all the available evidence was pooled and re-examined, had found that Garlic did have cholesterol lowering properties.

And highlighted the need for more independent studies into any Cholesterol lowering effects of Garlic.

For example, in one previous study of 220 patients who took 800 milligrams of powdered garlic for 4 months, the group experienced a 12 percent drop in cholesterol and a 17 percent drop in triglycerides as compared to the control group who took a placebo and experienced little change.

So again, the evidence is mixed, but the latest research does cast doubt.

It should be noted however that this study did not look at other purported health and heart benefits of eating garlic such as an anti-inflammatory effect, anti-cancer properties or a purported ability to lower blood pressure. So it does serve to remind us that with herbal remedies there is often a synergistic effect on total health that is worthwhile, even if individual components are not well proved.

Garlic of course does not need to be taken as tablets. It can also add flavour to meals. So, if you want to enjoy flavourful low-fat meals, than using garlic rather than salt or fats will help you stay healthy. Many health experts consider garlic to be a super-food that is generally beneficial for overall good health, and so regardless of the current debate over its cholesterol benefits it is a good addition to any diet.

Omega 3 Fatty Acids

Typically found in fish. But also in high quantities in certain seeds such as Flax Seed, Hemp Seed, and other non-animal based foods such as Soybean, Wheat Germ, Canola and Walnut Oils. (So even if you are a vegan or vegetarian, and don't eat fish, it is still perfectly possible to have good levels of Omega 3 Oils in your diet.)

Omega 3 Fatty Acids have been shown to be beneficial for heart health and brain function as well as being recommended for pregnant women. But here I will focus on the heart benefits that have been reported.

Dr. Fran Hu of the *Harvard School of Public Health* has published studies that suggest that high consumption of fish (4 to 5 times a week) cuts the risk of women dying from heart disease by 45 per cent compared to women who rarely ate fish.

Men with the highest levels of Omega 3 fatty acids have an 81 per cent lower risk of dying suddenly than men with the lowest levels. The fat in fish lowers cholesterol, helps prevent blood clots that form in heart attacks and lessens the chances for the irregular heartbeats that cause sudden deaths.

If however you are a Vegetarian or Vegan and so cannot consume Fish you can still consume Flaxseed Oil supplements which have the advantage of being animal free, but are also rich in Omega 3 and Omega 6 Oils. One gram daily of an Omega 3 fatty acid supplement has been reported to cut risk of sudden cardiac death by 42 per cent.

Flaxseeds

One study at *Oklahoma University* gave supplements of ground flaxseed to 38 women with extremely high cholesterol levels. After six weeks of eating muffins and bread containing 38 grams of either sunflower or flaxseed four times daily, their levels were re-tested. Their total cholesterol had reduced by 6.9% and LDL Cholesterol had reduced by 14.7%.

Beta Sitosterol

When taken at 300 mgs twice a day will help to lower blood serum cholesterol and triglycerides, even with few diet changes and little or no exercise. (Avocados are also naturally high in Beta Sitosterol, so you could also try eating more of those)

Psyllium Seeds

These seeds are a common ingredient in bulk laxative products. Studies have shown that psyllium can lower LDL cholesterol. With a study in May 2005 particularly investigating its role as an add on treatment to patients also taking a form of Statin (which I'll discuss later) called Simvastatin. This study showed that the dose of Simvastatin (a commercial drug treatment for high cholesterol) could be lowered by half (from 20mg to 10mg) if 15 grams of Psyllium was also added in.

This research is important because it identifies a continuing trend for research into Cholesterol treatments; where commercial drug treatments are compared alongside other therapies to try to find whether some work better together.

In this case the study concluded –

"Psyllium soluble fiber should be considered as a safe and

well tolerated dietary supplement option to enhance LDL Cho-
lesterol Lowering".

Soy Protein

A report in June 2000 in *Heart and Health Reports* summa-
rised the results of 38 recent studies of the effect of Soy on Cholesterol. It found that an average intake of 46 grams of Soy Protein per day reduced total cholesterol by an average of 9 per
cent, LDL Cholesterol by 13 per cent and Triglycerides by 11 per
cent. Some studies also showed that Soy raised HDL Cholesterol. And that for the patients who had the highest levels of cholesterol; it also had the greatest cholesterol lowering benefits.

To achieve the best results, eat at least four servings of
6.25 grams of soy protein or 25 grams per day. Countries that
enjoy diets rich in soy proteins, and this includes countries
such as Japan, have populations that suffer less from cancers,
heart disease, and high cholesterol.

Many Vegetarian 'Fake' Meat products are made of soy
protein, so this can be an easy and tasty source of soy protein if
you look for it in your local supermarket.

Women in countries that have soy-rich diets seem to be
less affected by osteoporosis and other dangers of menopause.
In fact, the countries that have traditional diets high in soy
have populations that seem to enjoy longer and healthier lives.
This has led researchers to investigate the potential benefits of
soy, and many research studies have found that soy proteins
seem to contribute to heart health and good overall health.

Other remedies believed to help reduce LDL choles-
terol include:

Vitamin E and C

Green Tea
Liquorice Extract
Aspirin (80 mg a couple of times per week)
Extra Virgin Olive Oil (1 tablespoon daily)

Questions to Ask a Natural Health Practioner

Herbs and other natural medicines and treatments are best recommended by natural or holistic specialists as many conventional doctors and specialists may not know a lot about herbal remedies. Some that do may not believe in their healing properties.

Your doctor may be able to recommend a natural health practitioner, as this field gains increasing credibility in the medical world. However, you may need to seek out a natural or holistic specialist yourself. This can be challenging, as there are fewer professional bodies regulating these experts. To make sure that you find an expert who can really help you, try the following:

1) Ask for recommendations from friends and family, especially if they have had success with holistic experts in treating heart and cholesterol issues.

2) Look for holistic specialists that have some formal training and certification. Many holistic trainers now have medical degrees as well as some training in holistic medicine. Some even do research work.

These sorts of holistic practitioners may be harder to find, but they are well worth finding, as their advanced training will help ensure that you get good healing treatments that also work in harmony with other medical conditions you may have.

3) Always speak to holistic practitioners in a pre-interview before agreeing to accept their services.

During this pre-interview, make sure that the natural practitioner listens to your specific circumstances, have a good knowledge of medicine and are qualified.

Ask for references.

Be wary of natural practitioners that make grandiose claims, seem to advertise one brand of products heavily, offer advice that contradicts basic knowledge about human health, or are vague or unhelpful when answering your questions.

4) Make sure that your Doctor knows which natural treatments you are taking before you take them.

Natural and herbal products may still interact with your other medications.

And if you have allergies or reactions to specific products or treatments then it is important to make sure that new treatments don't make the situation worse.

Keeping your doctor informed will make it easier for your doctor to help you, and safer for you.

5) Always ask for detailed labels or ingredient lists for all natural or holistic medicines or treatments you take. Read these carefully and check to make sure that you are not allergic to any of the ingredients.

It is important to not blindly "self-doctor" as herbs are potent and some people will react adversely to certain herbs and supplements.

Herbs and plant-based substances can be allergens and can still produce side effects, reactions, and interactions with other medicines.

Herbs are not recommended as alternatives to conventional medicine without professional guidance. Always consult with a trained professional for best results and make sure that you keep your Doctor in the loop as to what you are doing.

Pharmaceutical Medicines and Treatments for Cholesterol

If your doctor has found that you have high cholesterol, you will likely be advised to follow a low saturated fat and low cholesterol diet. You will also be told to exercise more and maintain a healthy body weight. Many doctors will encourage you to try these diet and lifestyle changes first because they have been proven most effective in controlling cholesterol and because cholesterol-lowering medications are strong drugs that may have side effects.

I have already spoken about many different health, food, nutrition and dietary changes that are available to you to try to lower your cholesterol and increase your overall heart and general health.

If after a number of months these diet and lifestyle changes have not lowered your cholesterol sufficiently, though, your doctor may suggest more aggressive treatment, which may include cholesterol-lowering medication.

If you have been advised by your doctor to take cholesterol-lowering medication, you will certainly want to understand your medication and the other cholesterol medication choices available to you. This will allow you to make better informed choices about your treatment.

In general, the most popular cholesterol-lowering medications used today include:

Statins

Statins are drugs that work by constraining the enzyme *HMG CoA reductase*. This enzyme regulates how quickly cholesterol is produced in the body. By slowing this enzyme, Statins are able to lower LDL cholesterol levels more effectively than many other cholesterol drugs currently on the market.

In fact, some studies have suggested that these cholesterol-lowering drugs can lower bad cholesterol by up to 60%, which can be very good news for people with severely elevated LDL Cholesterol.

Some studies have also shown that Statins may contribute to lowering triglyceride levels and even slightly increasing HDL Cholesterol levels.

All these benefits make statins among the most commonly used drugs for lowering cholesterol.

The Statins most used today are:

•Pravastatin (marketed as Pravachol or Selektine)
•Fluvastatin (marketed as Lescol, Canef and Vastin)
•Lovastatin (marketed as Mevacor and Altoprev)
•Simvastatin (marketed as Zocor) and
•Atorvastatin (marketed as Lipitor).

If you take statins to lower your cholesterol, you can expect to see results in a few weeks. You will have to take your medications at night, with food.

Some of the more common side effects patients may experience when taking Statins are, cramps, gas, stomach upset, constipation and other digestive problems.

In many cases, these symptoms go away by themselves or at least become less severe as the body adjusts to the statins.

In some case, your doctor may suggest taking a lower dosage in order to control side effects.

More serious complications from statins include the risks of muscle problems and liver problems. These complications are quite rare in patients who take statins, but if you notice any pain or unusual symptoms while taking them, you will want to seek medical help right away.

Bile Acid Sequestrants

Bile acid sequestrants such as Cholestyramine, Colestipol, and Colesevelam attach themselves to the bile acids in the intestine that contain cholesterol. The body can then get rid of the cholesterol in bowel movements rather than absorbing it. These drugs tend to lower LDL cholesterol 10 to 15%. And are often combined with statins for more effective treatment of high cholesterol.

If you take these drugs to lower your cholesterol, you must take them with water or fruit juice and with food. If you take other medication, you will have to be careful to take those medications one hour before, or several hours after the bile acid sequestrants, as these cholesterol-lowering medications may affect how other drugs are absorbed by your body.

Your doctor will have to advise you when to take your other medications to ensure that these cholesterol medications do not affect your treatment of other health conditions.

Usually, bile acid sequestrants are prescribed in doses meant to be taken once or twice a day.

If you take these cholesterol-lowering medications, you need to drink plenty of water, as many patients experience unpleasant symptoms such as gas, nausea, constipation, and a feeling of bloating when taking bile acid sequestrants.

Cholesterol Revitaliser

Fibrates

Fibrates decrease triglyceride levels and raise HDL Cholesterol. They are less effective in lowering LDL Cholesterol and for this reason are used more often by people who have heart disease rather than high cholesterol. However, in some cases, they are given in conjunction with cholesterol-lowering drugs to keep a patient's heart healthy while lowering cholesterol to acceptable levels. Fibrates that are often prescribed to lower cholesterol include drugs such as Gemfibrozil.

Usually, Fibrates are taken in the morning and at night, about half an hour before eating. Among the most common side effects of these drugs are stomach ailments, a higher risk of gallstones, and an effect on medications being taken to thin the blood.

If you are taking medications intended to thin the blood, your doctor will want to take special precautions if you are also being prescribed fibrates.

Hormone Replacement Therapy

Hormone replacement therapy is a hormone therapy meant to treat the symptoms and health effects caused by menopause in women.

It usually involves taking oestrogen ('estrogen' in the US) or a combination of oestrogen and progestin. This is meant to offset the risks that occur when women's production of oestrogen drops after menopause.

Among the effects of hormone replacement therapy is a lowering of bad cholesterol levels, which often rise in postmenopausal women.

Among the other benefits of hormone therapy is a reduction in instances of hot flashes and a reduced risk of osteoporosis and heart disease, some of the most common risks to meno-pausal and post-menopausal women.

However, experts disagree about whether hormone re-placement therapy is as effective as other cholesterol-lowering drugs in reducing bad cholesterol-levels in women.

To make things even more complicated, hormone re-placement therapy has also come under fire for adding to the risk of some cancers, gallbladder disease and blood clots as well as other potential risks.

Women should speak to their doctors about the risks and potential benefits of hormone replacement therapy in or-der to determine whether the treatment is appropriate for them.

Other Drugs

Some doctors may prescribe drugs meant to offset or treat heart disease as well as lower cholesterol. Some doctors, for ex-ample, may suggest that patients take obesity medications in-stead of cholesterol-lowering medications because obesity may be perceived to be responsible for the higher cholesterol levels.

In many cases, if any underlying condition is causing the elevated cholesterol, that condition may be treated to improve cholesterol levels as well as overall health.

It is important to remember that cholesterol-lowering medications are not a complete solution in themselves. Even if you are taking doctor-prescribed cholesterol medication, you will still need to:

• Control conditions such as diabetes, smoking, high blood pressure, and other health aspects that may affect your choles-terol and heart health

• Follow a diet that is healthy, low in salt and saturated fats, and low in food cholesterol
• Follow a good exercise regime
• Lose weight if you are not at your ideal weight

These heart-healthy choices may reduce or eliminate your need for cholesterol-lowering medications. Even if they do not, by following these simple steps you will help your medication work more effectively, ensuring that your cholesterol is under control more quickly.

Cholesterol medication alone does not usually work to reduce bad cholesterol levels and increase good cholesterol levels. Your best plan for that is to follow a lifestyle that is healthy.

Gene Therapy

Dr. Nicolas Duverger of Gencell in France along with *Dr. Caroline Desurmont* of *Institut Pasteur* in Paris are conducting studies associated with gene therapy.

In addition to their hope to find a good solution to reducing high cholesterol, they are also studying the elimination of fatty plaques associated with hardening of the arteries.

In the future, medical research being done now may provide more effective solutions to elevated cholesterol levels. In the meantime, however, there are a number of ways you can use today's newest products and innovations to lower your cholesterol.

Super Foods

To effectively lower high cholesterol there are a number of key lifestyle changes that can be made, especially to your food and diet. There are several new products and innovations that can help you with this goal:

Fats/ Margarine

If you can become accustomed to a lower fat diet you will be well on your way to better health.

New Products to Watch for include:

Benecol® margarine will lower cholesterol by some 10% when used as recommended. It contains sterols derived from pine tree wood pulp; elements which research suggests could help those with high cholesterol. This margarine will not affect your HDL or "good" cholesterol.

In the UK there is a product called **Flora Pro-Activ®** which is a margarine that works in a similar way.

Take Control® margarine and salad dressings are made from plant sterols which are soy based. These contain sterols which block cholesterol. These sterols have been found to help lower LDL cholesterol levels (bad cholesterol) even in those patients who are already taking statins as cholesterol-lowering drugs.

Avocados

Avocados are very high in fat, 32% fat in fact, and so you might conclude that if you are trying to lower your cholesterol that you should be avoiding them.

Right?

Well, actually no. Quite the contrary is true.

The reason is that avocados actually help to raise the levels of good HDL Cholesterol, whilst lowering levels of bad LDL Cholesterol. There have actually been specific studies into how avocados can lower your cholesterol quite significantly. *"How come? If the fat content is so high?"* You might reasonably ask.

Well, there was a study by *Dr David Colquhoun* in the *Wesley Hospital* in Brisbane, Australia reported in 1990 where they found that eating avocados daily for three weeks improved total blood cholesterol in middle aged women by 8%. Whilst their HDL Cholesterol level actually increased by 15%.

This compared to a control group who went on a low-fat diet for the same period, and experienced a reduction in total cholesterol of 5%. So both methods worked. But the avocado diet worked better.

It should be stressed that the women weren't living on just Avocados for the period.

Their consumption ranged between half an avocado a day for smaller women, and 1 and a half for heavier ladies. So it was easy to stick to for the participants without getting sick of avocados!

The study concluded that simply by adding avocados into your diet you could cut the risk of heart attacks by between 10 and 20 per cent, and cut death rates by between 4 to 8 per cent in 3 to 5 years.

The reasons for this seem to be that in addition to the high levels of monounsaturated fats in avocado. 63% of the fat in avocados is monounsaturated fat. Avocados also have high levels of Beta-Sitosterol, a type of Plant Phytosterol which you will also find is the ingredient in some new 'Cholesterol Lowering Spreads', which at a dose of between 2 and 2 and a half grams a day (2 grams is about the weight of a single Malteser) of Plant Sterols (higher doses haven't increased the effect) have been shown to reduce LDL Cholesterol by 10 to 14 per cent.

They help to reduce the amount of cholesterol absorbed from food into the body.

Interestingly, despite the fact of how high in fat and calories avocados are, most people on the study actually lost weight.

Exactly why is not clear. *Dr Colquhoun* has suggested that avocado contributes to a speeding up of the metabolic rate. However, that hypothesis has not been proved one way or the other (so don't start on a ten avocado a day diet! You can definitely have too much of a good thing).

However, avocados do serve to remind us that a dogmatic approach to the idea that low fat foods must always be best for us, may on occasion actually be doing a disservice to certain foods. As fat levels do not always tell the whole story.

We need to dig deeper and find out the kinds of fat. Avocados also have 60% more potassium than bananas and are rich in B vitamins, as well as Vitamin E and Vitamin K and C. So they are incredibly rich in nutrients.

So, rather than reaching for the bread and expensive *Plant Sterol Spread*, you may well be better to reach for the avocados and also get the other goodness and taste that it has to offer.

Other sources of natural plant sterols are found in corn, wheat and soy.

Nuts

Nuts such as almonds, pecans and walnuts have high amounts of monounsaturated or polyunsaturated fat so this helps to lower cholesterol. New studies have suggested that eating nuts, and especially almonds with the skins, may be beneficial for those who have elevated cholesterol. In fact, if you want to lower your cholesterol, get more of your daily fat intake from non-animal fats and less fat intake from animal proteins.

Oats and Barley

Oats and Barley have a soluble fibre known as Beta Glucan and this is key to lowering cholesterol. Research about barley and oats has suggested that these two foods may be beneficial in helping those with high cholesterol. To gain the best cholesterol lowering effects consume from two to four cups of dry oats or barley daily.

An April 2007 meta-analysis of 8 studies that included grains, was published in the *Cochrane Database of Systematic Reviews*. These studies looked at the effect of whole grain foods on Coronary Heart Disease.

In 7 of the 8 studies which used oats it found a reduction in total cholesterol and LDL Cholesterol of roughly 7 milligrams per deciliter after a period of between 4 weeks and two months of consumption.

So, a good first practical step to lowering you cholesterol is simply to change your breakfast to having porridge oats every morning. It is actually quite tasty and makes for a good warm and filling start to the day.

Fruits and Vegetables

Fruits and Vegetables including apples, citrus fruit, berries, carrots, apricots, cabbage and sweet potatoes are very high in soluble fibre and pectin.

Eat at least five servings a day for good heart health. Many studies have repeatedly proven that fresh fruits and vegetables are excellent for maintaining overall good health and preventing many serious illnesses.

Flaxseeds

Flaxseeds contain alpha linolenic acid a polyunsaturated fat which has been shown in research studies to lower cholesterol while providing needed soluble fibre.

Olive Oil

Olive Oil has been shown to effectively lower blood cholesterol. Cold pressed extra virgin olive oil is considered to offer the best results. Using olive oil rather than animal fats can help lower your cholesterol and improve overall health.

Fish

Fish that contains Omega 3 polyunsaturated fatty acids prevents blood from clotting and lowers blood cholesterol. Research also suggests that omega-3 is good for brain function and overall good health.

Other Food Tips to Maximise Your Chances of Success

• When preparing foods adapt to healthful baking, roasting and grilling. Go for the low fat cooking oil sprays. Coat your pan to sear in the juices rather than frying.

• Limit the use of egg yolks by using two egg whites for every one egg yolk (for example in omelette's and cake recipes). You won't generally notice any difference and you will enjoy your egg preparations just the same.

• Adapt to 1% milk and then to skimmed milk. Try soy and rice milks and also cheese, sour cream and ice cream alternatives that use them rather than cow's milk. These make for delicious and healthy choices and also serve to give you new taste experiences.

• Try your local health food store, where many vegan choices, including no-milk substitutes are available.

How Lifestyle Changes Can Affect Your Cholesterol Levels

Eating differently and getting doctor-supervised cholesterol treatment will help lower your cholesterol. However, to stay heart healthy and to start lowering your cholesterol quickly, you will need to make some changes to your way of life in order to reap the maximum benefits. Luckily, a few easy-to-make changes are all that is needed to start reaping big cholesterol-lowering benefits:

Exercise

Your heart is a muscle, and like any muscle, it gets stronger with exercise.

You can protect your heart, even if you have high cholesterol, by exercising a little each day or every few days.

A simple daily twenty minute jog can do wonders. You may also want to consider joining a gym to make exercise more automatic. Try to find exercise that gets your heart working but which is not too strenuous.

Always make sure that you speak with your doctor before starting an exercise regime (you may need to ease into it gently if you are out of shape) and always choose an exercise that you enjoy so that you stick with it.

Another key factor with sticking to any exercise regime is establishing a routine. You will find that if you go at the same time (preferably every day), that you will soon feel pulled to do it in the same way that you feel pulled to brush your teeth, or make a cup of coffee first thing in the morning.

In August 2007 the *American College of Sports Medicine* and the *American Heart Association* updated their recommendations for adults with regards to exercise.

The primary recommendation being that all healthy adults aged 18 to 65 need moderate intensity aerobic endurance physical activity for a minimum of 30 minutes on five days each week, or vigorous intensity aerobic physical activity for a minimum of 20 minutes on three days each week.

They defined 'moderate intensity' as a brisk walk that noticeably raised the heart rate. And 'vigorous intensity' as jogging that causes rapid breathing, and substantially raises the heart rate.

They also recommended performing activities that maintain or increase muscular strength and endurance for a minimum of two days each week. And defined this as 8 to 10 exercises with 8 to 12 repetitions of each of a progressive weight training program, or similar resistance exercises, such as stair climbing or weight bearing calisthenics, that used the major muscle groups.

They estimated that in 2005 in the United States, 23.7% of adults reported no leisure time activity at all. And that taken as a whole in 2005 more than half of all adults in the United States, 50.9% to be exact, failed to meet these guidelines. With the numbers roughly the same for men and women. (Men having the slight edge on activity, 50.7% meeting the guidelines, as opposed to only 47.9% of women. But hardly enough to claim victory in the exercise battle of the sexes ☺).

Here is what the study listed as some clinical benefits of exercise that have been noted:

"Disease outcomes inversely related to regular physical activity in prospective observational studies include cardiovascular disease, thromboembolic stroke, hypertension, type 2 diabetes mellitus, osteoporosis, obesity, colon cancer, breast cancer, anxiety and depression."

I particularly like the next part. Where they are basically saying that the evidence that exercise is great for you is so compelling, that studies are only being used to judge by how much, not if, you should be exercising. Bottom line. You should be. Here we go:

*"Scientific evidence continues to accumulate, with more recent efforts focused on the nature of the relationship between physical activity and health, **rather than trying to determine if such a relationship exists**. This additional evidence includes compelling new data on women and more conclusive evidence on stroke, some cancers, and cognitive function".*

To translate from Geek Speak. This is like saying, *"We observe that Marilyn Monroe was attractive. We are now simply trying to figure out just how attractive she was."*

And did you get that last bit? It even makes you smarter. In fact, a study in the June 2006 issue of the *American Journal of Geriatric Psychiatry* found that just two weeks of lifestyle changes that included memory exercises, daily exercise, relaxation techniques and a healthy diet had to quote the study, *"Highly significant changes in brain function as measured by PET Scan, but no change in the control group"* on 17 healthy volunteers aged between 35 to 69.

And, guess what, a healthy diet and exercise are two primary components of lowering your cholesterol. So it's good news all round.

Let's get real for a moment though. Even the best, most thoroughly, 'tested for heart health exercise program', is useless unless you actually do it.

So if the very thought of going on an exercise bike or a cross trainer brings you out in a cold sweat. Or if your gym membership has gone unused for the last six months. Then simply do anything active that you enjoy.

Such as riding a bike around the local park, walking the dog briskly, or having a sociable game of tennis, and work that into your schedule so that you do it regularly.

It should be something you enjoy doing. It should not be seen as something that you have to do to lower your cholesterol. The benefits of exercise go so far beyond lowering Cholesterol that it is something you should be doing anyway.

It needs to become part of your day that is automatic. In the same way that spending 10 minutes to put on clothes before you go out is automatic. Exercise should be the same. It shouldn't be a daily mental struggle and battle of wills.

None of us have a daily internal debate along the lines of:

"Well, Do I choose to put on clothes today? My leg aches and I'm not sure I can be bothered to lift it up. I did it yesterday after all. I think I'll stay in bed."

That would be a bizarre conversation to have with yourself wouldn't it? And yet people do this every day with their exercise routine.

"Oh well. I just don't feel like it. I don't have the time today. I

think my leg is playing up. Missing one day won't matter. I'll start again tomorrow."

Stop kidding yourself. Exercise needs to become a habit. It needs to become something that you, 'Just Do'. No big deal. You don't do a song and dance because you raised enough energy to put your pants on in the morning. And your exercise should be the same.

Take a leaf out of the Adidas Ad, and, *'Just Do It!'*

Some people find that varying their exercise routine and trying new forms of exercise makes it easier to stay motivated. Consider trying walking, hiking, swimming, yoga, horseback riding, bicycling, jogging, rollerblading, ice skating, skiing, rowing, or other activities that are low-impact and heart-healthy.

A Fitness Plan

Go get the equivalent of the yellow pages in your area, Google some choices on the internet, or visit a local library to see what local clubs are available in your vicinity that are activity based and actually require you to move!

I'm not talking about the local wine tasting group here, or the computer society. I am talking about local groups like walking clubs, tennis clubs, badminton groups, soccer clubs and baseball where sweating isn't optional.

Then take the step of phoning the person in charge and say this:

"Hi, I used to love baseball, badminton, tennis (whatever it is). And would really like to get started again. Can you tell me a bit about your club?"

They will then tell you the meeting times.

Try to find a club that meets at least once a week.

Rinse and repeat this strategy until you find that you are "exercising" several times a week, but that because you enjoy it, you will actually look forward to taking part, and not dread it.

Here is a massive list of sports on Wikipedia to get you thinking about the possibilities:

http://en.wikipedia.org/wiki/List_of_sports

American 19th Century Author, *Henry David Thoreau* wrote in Chapter One of his book '*Walden*' (**http://en.wikipedia.org/wiki/Walden**) –

"Most men lead lives of quiet desperation....
Observers and not active participants in their own destinies."

Do not be among them.

Make sure that you embrace the bold, but worthwhile endeavour of retaking control of your physical freedom by seizing the day and trying out some new activities.

In the same chapter of the same book Thoreau says:

"In the long run men hit only what they aim at. Therefore, though they should fail immediately, they had better aim at something high".

Aim high for your health.

Exercise doesn't have to be a solitary chore in a gym. It can be sociable and fun.

Exercise Facts

Here are some facts about exercise to really get you motivated:

A May 2007 study in the *Archives of Internal Medicine* concluded that, based on an average of 3.7 exercise sessions per week each lasting 40 minutes, the effects of aerobic exercise resulted in a 2.53 milligram per deciliter increase in HDL Cholesterol levels.

With each 1 milligram per deciliter increase in HDL Cholesterol levels being associated with a 2 to 3 per cent decreased risk of cardiovascular disease.

Exercise, by rough estimates could result in a 5.1% in men and 7.6% in women, reduction in cardiovascular disease.

A review of 36 studies of cancer and quality of life found that aerobic exercise during or following cancer treatment resulted in improvements in quality of life, exercise capacity, flexibility, body composition, fatigue, and muscular endurance. Pain, nausea, diarrhoea, sense of control, depression, self-esteem, and life satisfaction were also improved.

And finally one for the men over 50 out there...

Studies have shown that physically active men over 50 have a 30 per cent lower risk of impotence than their inactive counterparts.

Hopefully by now you have got the point.

Don't intellectualise about Exercise.

Just Do it!

Reduce Salt

Sodium products can cause hypertension and other conditions that are dangerous for those who already suffer from high cholesterol.

An April 2007 study concluded that reducing salt consumption by about 25 to 30% resulted not only in lower blood pressure, but also reduced the risk of cardiovascular disease by 25%.

So start paying attention to how much salt you add to foods and how much salt is contained in the foods you eat. You will be amazed at how much salt is added to most food before you have added anything.

You likely don't even notice the salt in your meals, since a taste for it is cumulative, the more salt you eat, the more you crave the taste, and the more salt it takes for you to enjoy your food.

In fact, once you have lowered your salt intake for a few months, you will likely notice that much of the food you used to like is far too salty!

You can add flavour instead of salt by adding raspberry vinegar, fresh herbs, garlic, peppercorns, and vegetable broth (sodium-reduced or homemade with no salt) to food. These same flavourings can be used instead of salt for a healthier meal.

You can also find salt-free and sodium-reduced products at your grocery store and local health store. These make a nice alternative to your usual high-salt products.

Maintain Your Proper Body Weight.

Keeping your body at its ideal size will help control cholesterol.

The good news is that eating more healthily sets you immediately on the right track to achieving this.

A frequent method that is used to determine your correct weight is to refer to a Body Mass Index Chart.

You can learn more about Body Mass Index here:

http://en.wikipedia.org/wiki/Body_mass_index

Drink Plenty of Water

Doctors agree that keeping yourself healthy by drinking lots of water is an important part of keeping your body functioning well overall. Besides this though, drinking water will make you feel full so that you don't overeat. Plus, drinking water instead of high-salt and high-sugar drinks will keep you healthier.

The first thing you should do every morning is consume a large glass of water. It will help to replace any water lost through overnight sweating, and really helps to kick start the system for the new day. You should also have several more glasses spread throughout the day.

There is no need to go overboard with this, but the colour of your urine is generally a good indicator of how hydrated you are. The more corn/yellow coloured it is the more dehydrated you are.

Spread your drinking throughout the day and avoid drinking with meals if possible as this dilutes stomach acid and may make digestion more difficult.

Stop Smoking

Smoking puts a terrible strain on your heart and lungs. You simply cannot be heart-healthy if you smoke.

Smoking is a risk factor for cancers, heart disease, and high cholesterol.

The *Framington Offspring Study* investigated cigarette smoking and HDL Cholesterol in 4107 men and women and found that cigarette smoking was found to be associated with an average difference in HDL cholesterol of about 4 milligrams per deciliter of blood in men and 6 milligrams per deciliter in women. And further studies have backed up this research and even suggested higher figures.

The *Lipid Research Clinic Program* in 1980 examined 2663 men and 2553 women between the ages of 20 and 69 for the same factors.

It found that men who smoked more than 20 cigarettes a day had HDL Cholesterol levels that were 5.3 milligrams per deciliter of blood, or 11 per cent, lower than those for non-smokers.

And women who smoked 20 or more cigarettes a day had HDL Cholesterol levels 8.6 milligrams per deciliter or 14 per cent lower than non-smokers.

The study concluded that cigarette smoking is associated with substantially lower levels of HDL Cholesterol. (And remember that HDL Cholesterol is the good guy who we want to see more of.)

But putting Cholesterol to one side for a minute.

Smoking has so many bad consequences to your health that even if it wasn't a disaster area for your cholesterol (which it is) you should still quit.

Here are some **Not So Fun Facts to ponder about Smoking...**

☐ Cigarette Smoking approximately doubles a person's risk for stroke.
☐ Smoking causes about 90% of all lung cancer deaths in

women and almost 80% of lung cancer deaths in men.
☐ Cigarette Smokers are 2 to 4 times more likely to develop coronary heart disease than non-smokers.
☐ Current smokers are twice as likely to experience impotence as non-smokers.
☐ Smoking increases the risk of erectile dysfunction by around 50% for men in their 30s and 40s.

Now, you have probably heard statistics like that in the past. Indeed, the packets themselves have dire warnings like *'This Will Kill You'* and yet people still smoke.

In fact, *Dr Elliot Wineburg*, the Director of the *New York Stop Smoking Medical Center* at *Mt Sinai Hospital* has said that *'Nicotine is more addictive than heroin'*. So quitting is very far from easy. But nevertheless you should try.

A study published in 2004 in the journal *Addictive Behaviors* found that smoking also affected your intelligence.

The Study was led by *Lawrence Whally* of *Aberdeen University* in Scotland. It assessed the mental abilities of 465 people who had taken an IQ test at the age of 11 in 1947.

These people were then retested again between 2000 and 2002 when they were 64 years old; and it was found that smokers performed significantly worse in five different cognitive tests then both former smokers, and those who never smoked.

Even when social and health factors such as education, occupation and alcohol consumption were taken into account. Smoking still appeared to contribute to a drop in cognitive function of just under 1 per cent.

So, if you do smoke, then visit your Doctor to enquire about help with quitting. Or else check out these websites for advice on giving up.

UK
www.quit.org.uk
www.smokefree.nhs.uk

US
www.smokefree.gov

And, what about drinking?

Well the good news is...

Don't Be Afraid To Add A Glass Of Wine To Your Dinner Once Or Twice A Week

Research suggests that alcohol in moderate amounts can help to lower bad cholesterol levels and raise good cholesterol levels. Some research has also suggested that some forms of alcohol may reduce the risks of coronary disease and may even act as antioxidants.

This does not mean that you should take up drinking, however.

Other measures will have equally cholesterol-lowering qualities, without you having to consume alcohol (which in anything much more than a couple of glasses a week is plain bad for you).

Just don't assume that you must cut alcohol from your diet totally to lower cholesterol.

If you are taking any medications make sure to ask your doctor or pharmacist whether the medication will react with alcohol (it most likely will – alcohol and medicine really do not go together).

Watch Out For Coffee

Some studies have suggested that coffee may contribute slightly to higher levels of bad cholesterol while having no effects on good cholesterol levels if you drink more than a few cups a day.

If you can't give up coffee, at least make sure that you drink filtered coffee, as many studies have suggested that it is the coffee oils in coffee, called terpenes that may lead to elevated cholesterol levels. Also, do your best to cut back on coffee and drink it with non-fat or low-fat milk products.

Coffee and the fats in coffee cream will certainly not help you with your goal of lowering bad cholesterol levels.

In one study, researchers in Sweden found that people who normally drank filtered coffee experienced a small drop in cholesterol levels when they stopped drinking coffee for a few weeks.

But the risk does need to be seen in perspective.

The effect is much less than smoking, high blood pressure or being overweight has on your overall heart health. So you can still drink coffee and lower your cholesterol overall if you deal with other dietary and health factors. But it is something to be aware of.

Start A Herb Garden

Whether you grow a small herb garden in your yard or in a window box, having fresh herbs on hand can help you reduce the amount of animal fats and salt you add to your foods.

Fresh herbs can add plenty of flavours to your cooking and most contain a number of nutrients that are good for your overall health.

Plus, studies have shown that living in an apartment or home with live plants is good for your general health.

Stay Positive

Staying positive and happy with your life can reduce stress levels (which are detrimental to your heart) and can encourage you to take the steps you need to lead a full and active life. Plus, changing your lifestyle and eating habits in response to high cholesterol can potentially be emotionally draining. You need to see it as a positive life change, rather than an onerous one 'forced' on you by considerations of health.

Making an effort to look after your emotional health can make this process less daunting. If your emotions and moods swing wildly as you adjust to a cholesterol-lowering lifestyle and diet, seek out a therapist or speak with your doctor to find help.

Chapter 5
Dealing with Your Doctor and Eight Cholesterol Myths Exploded!

If you want to lower your bad cholesterol quickly and experience a lifetime of good health. You need to work effectively with health care professionals.

Communicating With Your Doctor

Communicating effectively with your doctors and health care providers is very important, since you need to give them information about your condition and symptoms which may help them treat you. However, in today's world, where many doctors and care givers are rushed and overworked, it can be difficult to communicate in the short time you have for your Doctor's appointment.

You can make it easier to communicate with health care workers by choosing the correct ones in the first place.

Choose a doctor and specialists you feel comfortable with and trust. These professionals should have credentials that make you feel that you are in good hands and should also genuinely listen to what you have to say.

If you feel that your concerns are not being taken seriously, there is no reason why you shouldn't find an expert who will listen and give you the care you need. Ask friends and family members for their recommendations or ask for a referral for a second opinion.

Ask Questions

Once you have found a doctor that you trust, don't stop there. Ask questions both of them and also other people.

Ask friends and family members about their experiences with high cholesterol, ask the nurses who take blood samples about the procedures of lab tests, and read the pamphlets and booklets that are offered for free at many clinics.

The more professionals and people you ask and the more information you gather, the better you will be able to use your time with your doctor productively. You will know the basics and will be able to ask more directed and focused questions in the time you have available.

As you start lowering your cholesterol over the next 30 days, commit yourself to understanding all you can about cholesterol and cholesterol treatments. Because research and knowledge will make you better able to take the steps you need to lower your cholesterol.

Come prepared for appointments. Do your research ahead of time, so that you do not spend the limited time you have with health care professionals asking basic questions such as "What is cholesterol?" which you can find elsewhere. (And hopefully have a pretty good idea of by now!)

Spend the time with your doctor raising concerns, asking for specific cholesterol information that is relevant to your particular case, and getting instructions about what to do next.

Keep a Health Journal

One excellent way to be prepared to speak with your doctor is to keep a journal about your health and cholesterol.

Cholesterol Revitaliser

Once your doctor determines that you have elevated levels of bad cholesterol, buy a plain notebook. In it, keep the facts and information you find about your medication, cholesterol, and treatments.

Note down important contact numbers, including contact information for your doctor. Keep track of all the things you do each day including diet, nutrition, exercise, and medical treatments that may affect your cholesterol.

In each day's entry, also note any unusual symptoms or concerns you may have. Keep a running list of questions you want to ask your doctor at your next appointment, and note the progress you are making.

Bring this journal with you when you visit your doctor. It will prove invaluable to your health care professionals in helping you develop a form of treatment that works for you, and also provide a visual re-enforcement to you that the measures you are taking are having an effect. (If they aren't then change them!)

The most important thing about keeping lines of communication open with your doctor is to keep persisting with your efforts and doing your part to help yourself.

Show up for appointments on time, voice your ideas and discuss research you have discovered, and follow the directions your doctor gives you.

If you are having trouble following a specific cholesterol-lowering treatment, whether it is because of side effects or lack of motivation, be frank with your doctor about this. Your doctor needs to understand what you are not doing that may be affecting your treatment. Often, your health care professional will be able to give you some tips for making the treatment more realistic for you or may be able to offer an alternative treatment for controlling your cholesterol.

Always be sure to tell your doctor about all medication, herbal treatments, vitamins, and over the counter products you are taking. These can influence your cholesterol medication and have an impact on medical tests you may take.

Doctor Question Checklist

There are certain questions that you need to have answered about your condition over the next 30 days from your doctor or from another reputable health care professional. If you want to effectively lower your cholesterol, it is important that you understand the answers to the following questions:

1/ What exactly am I being treated for and what is my condition and prognosis right now?

Never assume that high cholesterol is what you are being treated for primarily. Your doctor may be more worried about another condition that is related to high cholesterol, such as obesity, for example and may be focusing on that in order to help you achieve optimal health.

Understanding what you are being treated for can help you understand what you should be focusing on.

Getting the exact numbers and figures related to your condition, such as the actual cholesterol levels, can also help you keep track of your progress as you make the changes you need to make to become healthier.

2/ What are the details of the medications I am taking?

Get a list of the medications and treatments you are taking (including full medical names so that you can research them further yourself if so desired) as well as their risks, side effects, and exactly how they should be taken.

Ask about any ingredients or medications these drugs could react with, how these drugs should be taken (on an empty stomach, with food, or at specific times of the day?) And find out how the drugs should be stored. (Out of the light, in the fridge, at room temperature?)

Many pharmacies now provide complete printouts that tell you all about the medications you are taking. It is well worth your while to seek out a pharmacy or pharmacist that can give you detailed information about your cholesterol-lowering drugs and can answer all your questions about your medications. Also find out what you are supposed to do if you forget a dose or experience side effects.

3/ What symptoms should I be looking for that indicate that I should seek help right away?

Medication and treatments for high cholesterol carry risks, and having higher cholesterol carries its own risks as well. Knowing which symptoms indicate that you need to seek medical help fast and knowing where to seek that help can literally save your life.

Write down the symptoms you need to stay alert for (such as possible side effects to taking medications) and carefully write down what you need to do if you experience specific symptoms. Review this until you know it off by heart.

4/ What are the specific steps I need to take to improve my condition?

Your doctor can recommend specific steps and instructions that you can follow to improve your health. Whether it is a certain diet or a special treatment, knowing what is expected of you is important.

Write these down as goals to be met, and assess with your doctor what are reasonable time frames to see results, and what those results might be expected to be.

5/ What diet and exercise steps are right for me?

While a low-fat diet and moderate exercise can help lower cholesterol, your doctor can recommend detailed routines that can address specific issues in your medical history.

If you have diabetes or food allergies, for example, you doctor can help you determine exactly what exercise and diet plan may be right for you that also takes those into account.

6/ Who else can I talk to and what other resources are available to me?

Most doctors are aware of lots of resources, including books, pamphlets, support groups, and other specialists that can help you to lower your cholesterol.

I also include a list of resources in the final chapter of this book so you can explore further.

7/ Am I a candidate for other cholesterol treatments or tests?

Understanding which other treatments and tests may help you in the future, if not right now, can help you see the options you have for treating your high cholesterol. Often, simply by getting your doctor to explain why you are taking specific medications, you will better understand your overall health situation.

8/ What are my most recent test results?

Again, write these down so that you can see your progress and evaluate where your health is currently. It is very easy to forget where you have come from with regards to factors such as cholesterol.

Actually taking the time to write down your health progress is important.

Over time it will speak volumes for the health improvements you are experiencing.

9/ What's next?

Before you leave your doctor's office, you should always know what you should be doing next to improve your cholesterol levels and your health. Whether it is scheduling a follow-up appointment, waiting for the results of another test, or health, dietary or exercise changes that you need to make. Ensure that you know what the next step of your treatment is.

8 Cholesterol Myths Exploded

There are many myths out there about cholesterol. If you believe any of the following, you may be making uninformed choices that can sabotage your chances of lowering your cholesterol.

Cholesterol Myth 1: *I follow a good diet, so I don't need to get my cholesterol levels tested*

People who are overweight and consistently choose high-fat and processed foods (which are high in trans and saturated fats) may well have elevated levels of cholesterol.

However, there are other risk factors to consider. People who eat well may also have heightened cholesterol in some cases.

You should be tested for cholesterol if you:

• *Are older:* Cholesterol levels may rise with age.
• *Are a woman who has gone through menopause:* Lowered oestrogen levels after menopause have been linked to higher levels of bad cholesterol.
• *Are a smoker:* Smoking is a big danger to heart health and may affect cholesterol levels.
• *Are sedentary:* Lack of exercise has a detrimental effect on cardiac health and cholesterol.
• *Are someone whose family has a history of heart disease or high cholesterol:* High cholesterol in some cases is genetically determined.
• *Suffer from alcoholism:* Alcoholism has been linked to heightened levels of triglycerides and heart disease. Getting a cholesterol profile can help determine if your heart is at risk.

Cholesterol Myth 2: *I'm young, so there is no need to worry about cholesterol*

Many risk factors affect cholesterol. A family history of heart disease, obesity, lack of exercise, and poor eating habits may cause even young adults to develop dangerously high cholesterol.

Cholesterol Myth 3: *I'm on cholesterol medication, so my cholesterol is decreasing anyway*

Cholesterol medication should never be seen as an instant solution to high cholesterol. It is always meant to be used in conjunction with a healthy eating plan and heart-healthy lifestyle to achieve the full cholesterol lowering affects you desire.

In fact, many doctors will not even prescribe cholesterol-lowering medication unless a patient has tried to lower their cholesterol with healthy eating and exercise and has had no success with reducing cholesterol in that way.

Keep in mind that even the most potent cholesterol-lowering medications take time to work. Plus, many of these strong drugs have unpleasant or even dangerous side effects.

For these reasons, diet and lifestyle should be your first defence against high cholesterol, and medications should only be used to complement or supplement these positive changes in your life.

Cholesterol Myth 4: *I just need to buy foods that are labelled as "low-fat" or "cholesterol free"*

Many products labelled "cholesterol-free," "light" or "fat free" are still high in trans and saturated fats or contain more fats than healthier food alternatives.

For example, it is possible that sandwich meats, a highly processed food, is labelled as "light" to suggest that it has less calories than the regular product, but this food is still likely to contain all sorts of unhealthy fats and ingredients that are bad news for your heart.

If you want to choose foods that are good for you, choose foods that are low in fats in general and foods that are low in saturated and hydrogenated fats in particular.

Eating fresh fruits and vegetables, whole grains, nuts, lean meats and fish is always healthier for you than eating processed foods that claim to be "light" or even "cholesterol-free."

Cholesterol Myth 5: *Eating margarine instead of butter will lower your cholesterol*

Fats can contribute to raised cholesterol levels, and you especially need to be aware of saturated and hydrogenated fats. There are actually a number of margarines that contain these types of fats.

To truly lower you cholesterol, you must decrease the total amount of fat you eat and choose fats that are lower in trans and saturated fats.

Choosing margarine will not automatically help you lower your cholesterol. Choosing a margarine that is low in saturated and trans fats and is not hydrogenated, and which contains sterols to act on lowering your cholesterol, may be beneficial in small quantities for your heart health and your cholesterol level.

Choosing to use small quantities of very good extra virgin olive oil instead of margarine may be even better for your heart and cholesterol.

Cholesterol Myth 6: *High cholesterol only affects men*

Until menopause, it is true that women tend to have lower levels of bad cholesterol. However, women who have a number of cholesterol and heart disease risk factors (these include genetics, obesity, lack of exercise, poor food choices, smoking, and alcoholism) may still have elevated cholesterol.

After menopause, women actually often have higher levels of bad cholesterol. In fact, many women who have experienced menopause find that they develop high levels of bad cholesterol that diet and exercise alone can't fix.

If you are a pre-menopausal women with risk factors for high cholesterol or heart disease, get a cholesterol profile done.

After menopause, women should have their cholesterol levels checked regularly.

Cholesterol Myth 7: *Eating eggs is not bad for you because dietary cholesterol does not matter as much as people once thought*

This myth is both true and false. Eggs yolks do contain high levels of dietary cholesterol. One egg contains about 213 milligrams of cholesterol (keep in mind that for most healthy people the recommended limit for cholesterol consumption is about 300 milligrams daily).

If your cholesterol levels are very high, you will need to be more careful, and limit your consumption of eggs, or eat less egg yolks where all the cholesterol (and a good part of the taste!) is found.

Even if you are generally healthy, if you wish to enjoy more eggs you will have to take extra caution to limit your levels of dietary cholesterol in your other foods.

In general, you do not want to think of foods as "bad" or "good", as most foods can be part of your diet, and eggs contain lots of great nutrients.

However, if you have high cholesterol, you will want to be careful about your consumption of eggs or switch to predominantly egg whites only.

Cholesterol Myth 8: *I feel healthy and my doctor has not brought up the subject of cholesterol with me, so I must have low cholesterol*

There are no physical signs of high cholesterol. Sadly, for too many people, the first sign of high cholesterol or heart problems is a heart attack or stroke.

You need to take matters into your own hands and not rely on a doctor or any outward physical symptoms to determine your cholesterol level.

Doctors are often overworked and you need to take responsibility for your own health.

Get it checked regardless, and take steps to eat healthy foods and exercise.

Chapter 6
Three Insider Cholesterol Secrets

In this chapter we are going to look at three insider cholesterol secrets that can really help you to assist your children or
grandchildren understand cholesterol, and also further drill
down on getting your own cholesterol lowered.

Secret 1 – *High Cholesterol Doesn't Just Affect Adults. So
Think About Your Children As Well*

Many people assume that high cholesterol is a problem that
affects middle-aged (and older) adults only and so allow their
children to eat all the fatty convenience foods they want, assuming that their early diet makes no difference.

Nothing could be further from the truth. Many more
children today suffer from high cholesterol. In fact, the numbers of children who are taking cholesterol drugs is on the
rise! And some studies have suggested that a childhood of
poor eating choices can contribute to higher cholesterol later
in life.

Besides this, many of the eating habits learned in
childhood affect our eating choices when we are adults. Children who are used to eating high-fat foods and convenience
foods are more likely to make the same choices as adults.

Think about it. We are all creatures of habit. If you
were brought up on a farm and have always got up at 6am.
Then when you leave home do you suddenly start getting up
at midday?

Maybe. But I suggest, generally not. You literally become so hard wired to getting up early, that you don't even
question it later in life.

The same is true of the foods we eat.

Switching to healthy foods as adults may be harder for children who have made less than heart healthy food choices all their lives.

Now can you change and choose to get up at midday or eat healthier foods? Of course you can.

But my point is that unless you actively question your food habits and routines (which most people do not), then you are destined to go through your whole life on autopilot with food, (and everything else for that matter). Choosing what you have always chosen, and being resistant to change.

So the food habits that you learn as a child will often be with you for life.

For all these reasons, controlling food intake and lifestyle choices, even in early life, can contribute to life-long heart health and good cholesterol levels.

If you have children, you can help ensure that they make the right food choices that can help them with their cholesterol levels now and later in life. In fact, if you and other members of your family have high cholesterol, you need to introduce your children to cholesterol-healthy eating early. As your children may be at an increased risk of developing high cholesterol themselves.

Luckily, it's not that hard to teach your children how to make smart food and lifestyle choices that are heart-healthy:

Here are some suggestions to getting started:

9 Tips To Help Children Be "Food Smart"

1/ Teach your children about healthy eating and cholesterol

If you have high cholesterol yourself, you may want to speak to your children about this. Informed children are better able

to make smart food choices that can help keep their cholesterol levels healthy later in life.

2/ Let children make healthy food choices for themselves

Give your children some say about the fruits, vegetables and
other foods that they eat. Go through heart-healthy cookbooks with your children and let them help you decide what
recipes to try. Food should be fun, regardless of whether it is
healthy!

3/ Be careful of the food attitudes you convey to your children

Children pick up emotional cues from their parents. If you treat
a cholesterol-friendly diet as a type of punishment, your children will likely see it the same way. If your children see you
turn to fatty junk food when you are depressed or feeling
stressed, they will likely do the same thing.

Why wouldn't they? You are their role model after
all.

Many parents are fussy eaters and pass this on to their
children, which is a terrible disservice. Fussy eaters will simply
not try different healthy food choices because the foods are
"different."

Make a conscious decision to embrace new food in a
spirit of adventure. Not a sense of foreboding.

4/ Don't pass on your prejudices about certain foods to your children

Just because you don't like cabbage or sprouts doesn't mean
they won't love them. So don't colour their judgment by being
negative before they have even tried them.

5/ Do not reward children with food.

If your child does well at a sports event, social activity or gets great grades in school, do not take them to a restaurant or for take-out to celebrate.

Give them horseback riding lessons or let them choose a toy or favourite activity instead. Many parents are tempted to keep sweet foods such as cupcakes and candy for "special occasions" and "special treats". But this inadvertently makes children associate sugary foods with good times and vegetables with punishment or everyday life. Not a good plan for long term health.

If you instead teach them that activity equals fun and adventure, then most health issues will naturally take care of themselves. As they will lead healthier lives almost out of habit.

6/ Take your children food shopping especially when you are shopping for fresh produce

Let your children choose which vegetables, fruits, and other healthy foods they would like. Encourage your children to decide which fruits and vegetables look as though they might be tasty. Treat your produce shopping trip as an adventure and your children will be more likely to eat their greens without a fuss (especially if they chose them).

Stepping back a moment from what food tastes like, or what good it does you when you eat it. The very look of most fruit and vegetables is tremendously interesting. Especially if you are a child and aren't so jaded by having supposedly seen it all and heard it all before, when it comes to food (like many adults).

Fruit and vegetables are all different fun shapes, amazing colours, and all have different textures.

Intrinsically they are far more interesting than the regular shaped, homogenous, commercial products on the shelves in cans. So never dismiss them as *'Just a carrot'*, or *'Just a pepper'* in front of your children. Children pick up on you social cues and will inherit your food prejudices.

Imagine now if you had never seen a bright orange, stringy carrot or a bright yellow, bulbous pepper. The words *"Wow – That's Amazing'"* would be more likely to spring to mind. So treat them with that awe and talk them up in front of your children as not only great tasting, but really quite cool!

If you are excited, then they will be too. Because they pick up on your emotions as a guide to how they should feel about things. Food included.

7/ Monitor what your children eat

As a parent, it is your responsibility to make sure that your children eat three balanced meals a day that include foods that are low in fats and high in nutrients.

Reduce the amount of sugars and fats your children eat and limit or eliminate the junk food from their diets.

8/ Become involved in your child's school lunch program or cafeteria

Many schools offer less than healthy school lunches as well as vending machines full of sugary foods. At a number of schools, though, parents have banded together to force school boards to provide better foods choices for students. Use this as your inspiration to make sure that your child can make healthy foods choices in school.

One study published in the December 2005 issue of the *Archives of Pediatric and Adolescent Medicine* analysed the food related practices of 16 middle schools in the United States.

The practices that were analysed included allowing snacks in classrooms and hallways, using food as incentives and rewards, and sponsoring classroom and school wide fundraisers in which students sold food.

The leading researcher on the study *Martha Kubik*, found that for each of these practices that were allowed by a school the student Body Mass Index increased by 10%.

In other words, by allowing these practices we adults are contributing to childhood obesity. At a time when about 30% of American children, and 65% of American adults are overweight.

So the watchword has to be guidance. It is not enough to passively sit back and let your children eat junk food.

At least offer guidance, direction and a pattern of leadership in the food choices you make.

Where you lead, they will follow.

If you are worried about what your children eat, consider taking them to a nutritionist who can help teach them (and maybe you) what they should be eating.

Even if your child has elevated cholesterol levels, realize that growing children still need more fats and nutrients than adults.

Never simply place your child on a very low-fat diet. Consult with a Paediatrician to find a diet plan that can help your child grow whilst keeping their weight under control. A diet that is too low in fat may affect childhood development, so monitor it closely.

9/ Get your children to exercise

Virtually all health experts agree that North American children do not exercise enough. This has disastrous effects on heart health and overall health. One of the best things you can do to keep your children away from the dangers of high cholesterol is to get them to exercise at least a little each day. Find an activity they enjoy and encourage them to persist with that activity.

If your child smokes, is overweight, or has at least one parent who has a cholesterol level of more than 240mg per deciliter of blood, then they are at an increased risk of high cholesterol, even at an early age.

Take your child to the doctor, especially if your child has more than one of the risk factors for a complete check-up and cholesterol check.

Now we are going to look at two more secrets that can actively help you to lower your cholesterol.

Adopting a healthier lifestyle is often challenging, especially if you have followed less than ideal eating and life patterns for some time.

Although we may know which foods we should be turning to and which lifestyle changes we need to make, we don't always do what is right.

If you are inventing excuses or having a hard time sticking to the food plan your doctor or nutritionist has helped you develop to lower your cholesterol level, consider two secrets that can help make lowering your cholesterol over the next 30 days far less painful:

Secret 2 – *Avoiding Advertising Can Help You Lower Your Cholesterol*

It sounds crazy, but avoiding advertising can help you lower your cholesterol.

Why?

Think about it.

Why do you eat the way you do?

At least part of the reason has to do with learned behaviours. You learned to like some foods as a child, but you have also learned to associate certain foods with certain ideas and ideals and likely a good part of this has been the result of exposure to adverts on television and the media (both online and offline).

Do you associate beer with spending time with friends watching the big game on TV? Happy food parties for children with going to McDonalds? Mars Bars with working hard and playing hard?

Think about your own associations with food and ask yourself, *"Where did that come from?"*

Advertisers spend fortunes getting you to eat their foods. So is it any wonder that over time we are influenced to consume them?

Probably not.

If I ask myself the questions:

Who taught the world to sing in perfect harmony in their ads? And

What snack bar helps you work, rest and play?

Then I immediately think of a Coke and a Mars Bar. The perfect snack combination. Right?

Now, I haven't even seen those adverts on television for years. And yet even the thought of them stills triggers me to want to nip out and get a Coke and a Mars ☺, even though I know that there are certainly healthier things to eat.

So, think now of all the food adverts in YOUR experience that trigger you to go and get your next snack.

I bet there are quite a few.

Advertising even has the power to totally flip logic on its head.

The example that immediately springs to my mind is Tic Tacs. In the US they were advertised as *"The 1½ Calorie Breath Mint"*. In the UK, Ireland and Australia we got *"2 Hours of Tic Tac Freshness in less than 2 Calories"*.

Let's think about that for a moment.

That's PER Tic Tac!

They are only the size of the end of your fingernail.

To get that number into perspective, a whole carrot has just 30 calories and considerably better nutritional content.

And yet somehow the fact that each Tic Tac ONLY has 1 and a half calories, has been flipped on its head to be a good thing!

And we are being bombarded with this kind of advertising every day.

When you picture a hamburger, you likely picture the hamburger you see in the adverts. A large, juicy burger with all the toppings.

McDonalds. Burger King. Wendy's anyone?

When you think of a salad, you may not get the same strong images in your head, simply because salads and vegetables are advertised a lot less.

Think of the last ten food advertisements you have seen. Odds are, they were for less-than–healthy processed foods.

How many adverts do you see extolling the virtues of carrots, cucumbers or the like? Not too many.

Traditionally, less than healthy foods have needed advertising, because they were not needed. Today, though, there is a huge market for convenience foods.

When you visit your local grocery store, compare the amount of shelf space given to convenience foods, junk foods, sugary foods and sodas to the amount of space given to the produce section.

Sure they can taste good, and no-one is saying go and eat like a Buddhist monk. But in most grocery stores, the amount of space that fresh produce and fresh foods take up is far less than the amount of space devoted to less heart healthy foods.

This is no mistake. Take a look at those high-fat and cholesterol-high foods. Odds are, they come in brightly designed packages that grab the eye. Often, they are placed at eye level. They have massive marketing budgets pushing them and lots of smart people figuring out your psychological buttons to press to get you to try them.

So, what can you do about it?

Well, how about starting with your own:

Food Advertising Lowering Action Plan:

1) Reduce the amount of food advertising you see

Advertisers do an incredible job at making foods attractive, but many times these foods are less than great for your cholesterol level. There is no reason why your heart health should suffer because some advertiser is good at their job.

Figure out where you see advertisements for foods and then avoid those ads.

Most people see the majority of food advertisements on television. If this describes you, avoid the television for a while. Or get a hard disk recorder or Tivo Box (**www.tivo.com**) and fast forward over the ads, and watch your cravings for fatty foods decrease.

This strategy actually has the secondary advantage of also creating more time to do other things, because an average hour of TV now has many more unnecessary breaks then it used to.

Consider this from Wikipedia:

"In the 1960's a typical hour long American show would run for 51 minutes excluding advertisements. Today, a similar program would only be 42 minutes long.

A typical 30-minute block of time now includes 22 minutes of programming with 6 minutes of national advertising and 2 minutes of local.

In other words, over the courses of 10 hours, American viewers will see approximately 3 hours of advertisements, twice what they would have seen in the sixties" (**http://en.wikipedia.org/wiki/Television_advertisement**)

If you are able to fast forward through all those extra adverts, then you gain three hours out of every ten to do something more productive with.

Also avoid food advertisements in magazines and newspapers. That cream cake may look good on the page, but remember, it is going to end up as fat on your gut or thighs!

YOU should be deciding what you eat. Not having some desire emotion triggered because some guy in an advertising agency knows which of your buttons to push.

To illustrate. There was an interesting study published in March 2007 by the *Kaiser Family Foundation* called *'Food for Thought: Television Food Advertising to Children in the United States'*. It found that in 2005 children between the ages of 2 and 11 were exposed to a total of 20,000 paid advertisements on television EVERY YEAR.

And that of those 5,600 were ads for food. Or more than a quarter. That is an average of about 54 ads EVERY SINGLE DAY OF THE YEAR, of which 14 would be food ads.

If children are being bombarded with that level of food advertisements on television (and that doesn't even include other media like listening to the radio, billboards, or ads on the internet) from such an early age. Is it any wonder that they form strong associations with certain foods very early on?

And here is another thought to ponder.

You are seeing those ads as well.

How much of the food in your cupboards matches up with what the adverts have told you to buy?

Time to break free.

How about having a TV free week. Read a book. Walk the dog. Take up water-skiing. Whatever. Escape the bonds. Unplug the TV and set yourself free.

Here is a little challenge for you.

Watch no TV. Read no newspapers and stop listening to the radio for a week. And see how you feel.

You really aren't missing much. Other People's Lives are not as interesting as your own. So stop living as though they are.

The world is not going to radically spin off its axis in a week. And if you are that worried about missing the latest news, then ask the guy in the coffee shop if anything big has been going on, when you get your morning cup of coffee. You will soon realise when you unplug for a while, that the world seems to keep right on turning, whilst you just may be a little more relaxed.

You will free up a ton of time to do something considerably less passive, like sport, reading or a hobby you like. And at the same time not be bombarded with the avalanche of negativity and bad news that seems to be a normal day on the television and in the newspapers.

2) Make "good-for-you foods" appealing

Put your low-fat dinners on nicer china and eat at the table instead of in front of the television.

Use brightly coloured fruits and vegetables and arrange your heart-healthy food in an attractive way on the plate, much as restaurants do.

Add some music or candles to your dinner.

Any small and fast touches that can make your meal more appealing will make your new healthier food seem more like a luxury than anything else.

After all, this is exactly what restaurants do to advertise their food when you are actually in the restaurant. They add ambience and mood by the way the food is presented and the service you get to make the experience more pleasant.

In turn average meals seem more attractive and appealing in nice settings. So that customers are more likely to walk away feeling happy and satisfied with their meal, and hence come back for more in the future.

Good restaurants will often spend large budgets on consultants that can tell them what they can do to make the surroundings more appealing to customers.

Is it any wonder that restaurant meals, even those that are fatty and terrible for your cholesterol, are so hard to resist?

The great thing is that you can add this same type of "advertising" to your own heart-healthy meals.

Make them more appealing in any way you can think of and you will be amazed at how much easier your new eating plan is to stick to.

Have fun with it.

If you have a significant other than how about getting them to feed you strawberries? ☺

Make It Fun!

If a strawberry feeder isn't on hand, or isn't in the mood to play Cleopatra. Then go and buy some anyway and feed yourself some strawberries. Smile and feel good about yourself and celebrate the changes you have committed to make by getting *Cholesterol Revitaliser*.

Making food seem sensual and sexy is a sure fire way to make you want to eat it more often. So make the healthy option the appealing option.

3) Describe foods in ways that makes them more appealing to you

Advertisers work very hard to make sure that you remember jingles and descriptions of the foods that they advertise.

That is why you can often sing the slogans for popular advertisements years after the ads are no longer shown.

Sing along with me folks... *'I'd like to teach the world to sing in perfect...'*

Could you have completed that with the word 'harmony'?

If you can it is because you are remembering an advert for Coca-Cola. If you can't, then I am sure that there are plenty of others you would have known if you ever watched much TV as a child.

You can use the same technique to make good-for-you foods seem appealing. This is especially important since there are few ads for these foods and many of us come to associate negative images with health foods.

You likely have heard fresh fruit and vegetables described as "rabbit food" or as being "boring". This is not likely to make you crave these foods, especially since you are always hearing great adjectives such as "delicious" and "juicy" described about fatty foods.
Try to do the same thing as advertisers when buying food that is good for you.

Watch out for negative words.

Use words such as "crisp" and "delicious" to describe heart healthy and good-for-you foods.

Get into the habit of thinking positively about foods that are positive for you.

4) Use a little negative advertising

Whenever you find yourself craving foods that are high in fat or salt, use a little negative advertising.

As soon as you are aware that you are craving the foods, imagine them in your mind in the worst possible light, as mushy, greasy, cold, congealed, and disgusting, and this will immediately make them seem far less attractive.

If you find that you crave convenience foods, fast foods, and other foods you are trying to avoid during the next 30 days and beyond. Try to find ways to make these foods less appealing.

For example, recall the times you have had terrible fast food or convenience food meals. Ask your friends and family for their dining-out horror stories, and look up stories about the disgusting things people have found in fast foods and convenience foods.

Collecting and reading stories about the hairs and other unappetizing things that have been found in convenience food will make these foods seem far less attractive.

By making heart-healthy foods such as vegetables more attractive, you will find it much easier to stick to a healthy eating strategy, without feeling cheated or deprived.

And note, I am not saying "diet". This is not a diet. It is a health and life choice. The fact is that it is healthier, so you could lose weight if you wanted to. But it's not about that. You can generally actually eat more of cholesterol lowering friendly food like vegetables and fruit, because they tend to be lower in calories.

So you can lower your cholesterol and actually eat more if you want to. As long as you eat the RIGHT foods.

Secret 3: *Turn Low Cholesterol Foods Into Convenience Foods*

You should make cholesterol-friendly food choices easier on yourself than bad-for-you choices. That way you are far more likely to reach for low-fat, healthy foods on an ongoing basis. And are less likely to cheat on your new eating plan.

Let's now look at 16 ways that you can make this goal a reality.

16 Ways To Set Yourself Up For Cholesterol Lowering Success

1) Get rid of food temptations from your house

This can make a big difference. Out of sight is often out of mind.

I've touched on this before. But let's get specific.
If the snack food is not in your house, then you are immediately less likely to eat it, because it is more of a hassle to go and buy it , then it is to eat something else.

If you keep cookies, fried foods, and other temptations easily available, then you are more likely to turn to them when you are feeling hungry.

As soon as you learn from your doctor that you need to take care about what you eat because of elevated cholesterol, go through your home and get rid of the foods that you should be eliminating or cutting back on.

Replace your foods with healthier alternatives.

The same goes for any fliers, leaflets, or menus from local food take-outs and restaurants. Get rid of them. Re-cycle them. Just don't have them in your house.

If these things are not in your home, you are far less likely to be tempted by them.

Your local takeaway restaurant is NOT your friend if you are trying to reduce your cholesterol.

2) Make your kitchen a heart-healthy place

If you have a deep-fat fryer, give it away. Invest in parchment paper, non-stick cookware, a rice steamer, wok, or other appliances and gadgets that make heart-healthy and low-fat cooking more likely.

You do not have to invest a lot of money for this. Just buying parchment paper (for lining cooking pans) and getting rid of appliances that are only for high-fat cooking is often enough to make good low-fat cooking almost automatic.

While you are cleaning out your kitchen, try to find ways to make cooking in your kitchen more appealing. Hang up some nice curtains or at least get rid of the clutter.

If your kitchen is an enticing place to cook, you are more likely to cook at home rather than being tempted to eat out.

3) Eat in

As you strive to lower your cholesterol, you should eat in and eat foods you have prepared yourself as much as possible.

Ready-Meals and foods you buy from take-out restaurants and in restaurants do not give you as much control over ingredients and preparation as you have at home.

When you make your meals yourself, you can easily reduce how much fat and sodium goes into each meal.

The same is not true in a restaurant.

4) Get lots of appealing heart-healthy foods into your kitchen

If you make healthy foods more attractive and visible, you are more likely to reach for them when you are hungry. Buy pretty hanging bowls for your citrus fruits and vegetables instead of hiding them away in the cupboard.

Covered mesh containers are available for fruits. These containers allow fruits to ripen and stay visible, but prevent fruit flies.

The more "good for you" foods you have readily to hand and easily available, the better.

5) Consider taking a heart-healthy cooking class

Many community centres and cooking schools now offer cost-effective cooking classes in cholesterol-friendly and heart-healthy foods. This can be an excellent way to make healthy eating fun, especially if you feel out of place in a kitchen.

You will learn many recipes and cooking tips for heart-healthy eating, and have the opportunity to spend time with others who are concerned about eating healthy, but tasty food.

6/ Consider turning vegetarian

One good tip here is to contact your local vegetarian society, because by their very nature Vegetarians are forced to put fruit and vegetables top of the food agenda.

Ask them for recommendations for vegetarian cooking courses and spend some time learning to cook without high fat meat products.

You could certainly simply have less meat in your diet, but could also consider turning Vegetarian.

Here are Vegetarian Societies in the UK and US:

UK – Vegetarian Society:

http://www.vegsoc.org

Vegan Society:

http://www.vegansociety.com

US - List of Vegetarian Organisations:

http://www.vegetarian-restaurants.net /OtherInfo/Organization.htm

Vegan Society :

http://www.americanvegan.org/

If nothing else you will gain a new appreciation for the wide variety of foods that you may never have previously used, and it will give you new choices and options to preparing food in alternative ways.

When you prepare a meal, make sure that most of your plate is taken up by fresh fruits and vegetables. The portion size of grain should be smaller and the portion size of animal proteins (meats, milk products) should be smaller still.

It is a telling statistic that while the average cholesterol level in the United States is 210 milligrams per deciliter. The average vegetarian's cholesterol level is 161 and the average vegans cholesterol level is 133.

So cutting out animal products entirely can be a great strategy to lower your cholesterol dramatically.

7) Plan your cholesterol-lowering meals once a week

Most of us plan our days activities and our finances, but we often leave eating to chance. This can make heart-healthy eating more difficult. After a long day at work, it can seem daunting to come up with a menu and then cook a meal from scratch.

It is easier to reach for a microwave meal.

Knowing this, choose one day a week to plan your entire eating menu for the coming week and then go shopping for the ingredients you will need

This will ensure that you have all the fresh ingredients and healthy meal ideas you need, and if you plan them out when you are feeling energetic, it will be easier to get yourself to take action at the end of a day at work.

8) Get help in the kitchen

Whether you get help from a roommate, child, or spouse. Cooking with someone else tends to be more fun.

If you can't find someone to help you, then find some other ways to make cooking time more fun.

Listening to music or watching a movie on a portable DVD player as you cook, and cooking time will fly by.

Or how about buying some music or spoken books from *iTunes* or *Audible.com* and listening to those? You could get through a couple of new books every week while preparing nutritious and cholesterol-lowering meals for yourself.

9) Socialize without food

Many of us take in excess calories and fats when we eat out with others. This is especially a problem since we so often equate social times with eating. We meet friends at restaurants, coffee shops, and pubs or we have movie nights that include take-out pizza.

Make it a habit to meet friends at places that don't have food as a major source of the entertainment.

Meet friends at activity clubs, swimming, on hiking trails, or in your home rather than in restaurants or cafes that feature rich foods. If all else fails then meet at coffee shops, but order the orange juice rather than the bucket of coffee and a Danish ☺.

10) Get motivated

Getting started on healthy eating is often not the hard part. The hard part is staying motivated to keep it up for long enough to see results. So find ways to get yourself motivated to eat well for life. For many of us, unfortunately, fear is a greater motivator than the rewards of a healthy lifestyle.

If you have very high cholesterol, consider pinning your cholesterol level and a list of the dangers of high cholesterol on your fridge.

Or, put a really graphic picture of clogged arteries or some cholesterol health hazard you fear, where you will see it regularly.

The aim here is simply to sober you up to realities and act as a reminder of where you don't want to be.

You can kid yourself that what you eat, how much exercise you do, and that you smoke or drink regularly doesn't matter. Because most people either know about, or have heard of people who have lived long lives and done all of these things.

So hey, the same could be true of you, right?

Well, it is certainly possible. But the fact that some people can get hit by lightning several times and survive, doesn't make it a good strategy for most of us to stand in the middle of a field when a lightning storm is going on around us.

Far better to beat the odds by getting out of the storm in the first place.

You need to be realistic. And if reminding yourself of where you don't want to be works for you, then by all means use it to your advantage.

In the same vein you could also make a bet with a friend or family member that will see you lose money each time you cheat on your new healthy eating plan, don't go down the gym, or light a cigarette.

On the other hand, if you ARE motivated by good things, then how about posting a picture of what you would ideally look like on your fridge. Or else promise yourself a certain treat, such as a holiday, or a shopping trip if you achieve a certain health milestone.

Or maximise your chances and do both ☺.

11) Make heart-healthy food more convenient

As I spoke about earlier, if you can make low-fat alternatives easier to reach for than fast food, you are more likely to reach for meals and foods that are good for you as well as schedule-friendly.

Luckily, fruits, vegetables, and other low-fat foods are among the most convenient foods out there.

Keep cut up fruits and vegetables in your refrigerator to make stir-fries, salads, and other healthy meals easier.

Keep low-fat yogurt and other low fat foods around for fast snacking, and you can then reach for these foods rather than turning to high-fat, high-salt "fast foods."

12) Make heart-healthy food more interesting

You are unlikely to be satisfied with eating the same salad or the same types of healthy meals each day.

Sticking rigidly to the same sorts of foods will get you in a rut and will make high-fat alternatives seem more appealing.

Find new healthy foods that you enjoy, and make it part of your eating plan to look up new recipes and foods each week so that you always keep your diet interesting.

13) Figure out your eating dangers and find ways to overcome them

Most of us have specific emotions and events that may make us turn to comfort food.

Whether it is general stress, sadness, boredom, or meetings with your boss, it is important to find out which events cause you to overeat or to crave fatty foods, and then work hard to find alternatives.

Sometimes, this is very simple. If your walk home from work takes you past a favourite cafe you find hard to resist, then you may need to find a different route home.

If Tuesday work meetings leave you reaching for cookies in your office desk, find a way to get out of the meetings or take a walk after the meeting instead of reaching for food. (Or lock the drawer and give the key to someone else!)

Make a list of the times you are most tempted to eat, and beside each item, list ways you can avoid the situation or at least make better choices when you are faced with it.

Post your list in your planner or other visible place so that you will see it.

14) Make cholesterol-friendly eating easier

If counting fat grams, sodium, fibre, types of fat, and cholesterol in each of your foods is causing you stress, then you could get a small gadget that will count the grams and amounts for you.

You can even get programs for your computer or iPhone that will do this.

For example, **www.livestrong.com** sell an iPhone application that has a built in calorie counter and a database of over half a million foods.

You don't have to give up convenience. You just need to put a little thought up front and check a nutrition guide once (assuming you want confirmation that an apple is healthier than a doughnut).

Or, alternatively, simplify the process by eating more of the good stuff and less of the bad.

Sound too simple?

Not at all.

There are probably less than ten foods that you regularly snack on during the week.

Here is what to do

Make a list of the foods that you regularly snack on in between meals.

Now, next to each write down a healthy alternative that you could snack on that would be better for you, but that you could eat in an *'I don't need to think about it. I could just eat it'* kind of way.

So, for example, say you regularly have a doughnut every morning. How about replacing it with an apple, or a grapefruit?

Stick that list where you will see it and the next time its doughnut time instead look at the list.

Doughnut equals Small Salad.
Doughnut equals Pear...

Then don't use up sweat equity. You are hungry. So go and eat one of the alternatives you have written down in place of doughnuts.

If you absolutely love doughnuts (it could be chocolate cake or whatever) and still want to eat them occasionally. Then, you could operate your own personal version of one of those schemes that you see in coffee shops, where when you buy 10 coffees you get the eleventh one free.

Only in your scheme for every 10 *'healthy alternatives'* you get to have the *'naughty, but nice'* original treat.

Just make sure you don't gobble down the first ten quickly in order to get number eleven!

15/ Get a juicer

You should also think about getting a juicer or smoothie maker so that you can turn some of those vegetables and fruits into delicious and nutritious drinks.

Freshly squeezed orange juice fresh from the orange, as opposed to the stuff from the carton tastes immeasurably better.

And you can get really creative by combining different juices like carrot and apple.

You can experiment and try tasting different varieties of fruit and vegetables together. So if you are having problems eating your "five a day", then you could try juicing them as an alternative.

16/ Variety is the spice of life

Make sure that you eat a wide variety of food. Use olive oil as your main source of fat and refuse other dressings or sauces.

Eat much less of foods such as meats, full-fat dairy products, egg yolks, and convenience or restaurant meals and you should be able to lower your cholesterol significantly without counting every gram of food you place in your mouth.

Cholesterol Revitaliser

Chapter 7
The Cholesterol Conscious Chef
Goes Shopping

If you do most of your shopping at the local supermarket, are you often tempted by the foods you see on sale in the aisles?

The answer is obviously yes. Who isn't?
Where and how you shop can have a huge impact on your cholesterol levels.

Do you leave the store with high-fat items that were not on your list? Foods such as potato chips and frozen chicken dinners?

You are not alone.

The many foods and choices available to us when we shop should make it easier to choose healthy items that we enjoy and which are good for us, but the opposite is also true. When faced with lots of food choices, many of us find it hard to resist the foods that we know are bad for us.

Luckily, relearning to shop can go a long way towards lowering your cholesterol.

First, let's consider where you shop for food.

Food Shopping The Smart Way

1) Greengrocers, Farmer's Markets, and Farmer's Stands

These are excellent places to shop, and if you want to lower your cholesterol over the next month, you will want to make it a priority to shop at these types of locations for groceries if at all possible.

Your initial instinct may be that there aren't any farmers markets in your location. But don't be so hasty. If you search on Google for "Your location + farmers market" you will come up with a list very quickly.

Here for example is a list of farmers markets in New York:

http://www.nyfarmersmarket.com/

Here is one for Los Angeles.

http://www.farmernet.com/

Here is a list of Farmers Markets in the UK.

http://www.farmersmarkets.net/

You just need to look. There are a lot more of them then you might think.

Shopping at farmer's markets, farmer's stands, and greengrocers has several advantages:

• You will get a much wider variety of very fresh food products than you would get at a grocery store.
• You will support local farmers and often enjoy lower prices (though not always, sometimes you have to pay more for quality).
• These places are more environmentally friendly and give you better, healthier choices.
• They generally feature fewer or no advertisements for branded and convenience foods packed with fats.

If you want to lower your cholesterol and enjoy a healthier diet, shopping at your local farmer's market, greengrocer or farmer's stand is an excellent way to get the foods you need to stay healthy.

2) Farms and Organic Farms

Pick-your-own farms, organic farms, and farms that sell directly to customers offer great value and fresh in-season healthy foods, often at great prices.

A few hours at one of these farms can give you some fresh air, exercise, and the foods you need to stay healthy. It also makes a great afternoon activity to share with friends and family. Visiting these sorts of farms for some of your menu items is a great way to eat more heart-healthy products.

You can get a list of pick your own farms in the United States, Canada, Britain and Australia on this website.

www.pickyourown.org/

3) Health Food Stores

Health food stores often have a wide variety of products that are low-fat, healthy, tasty and good for you. Health food stores can truly be packed with unusual food gems.

They are often tucked away in obscure parts of shopping malls, and so you may miss them on a quick look.

But persist!

Go grab your local directory listings or hunt them down on the internet! They are pure gold!

Again, Googling "Your location + health food store" is the easy way to find these stores.

They can be great places to buy dried peas and lentils, herbs, natural products and a wide variety of items that are not available at your grocery store, but which are great for your heart health.

And, take note! Here is an example of where big is not necessarily better. Because these health food stores can often be quite small. But because of that, it means that you don't have to trawl through 57 aisles of your local Mega Supermarket to find the items that are actually designed to be good for you!

These places typically stock the products from smaller, more specialized food manufacturers, and hence often have items that you won't be able to find even in the supermarket.

This is especially true of lots of the Vegan lines (Don't dismiss them until you have tried them! Some of them are delicious). Which are often really great for heart health and for our goal here of lowering your cholesterol.

So, let your fingers do the walking for once, and as soon as you have finished reading this book, go and find at least one new Health Food Store that you have never visited before so that you can go and check it out.

4) Grocery Stores

Many grocery stores offer a produce section as well as meat and deli sections which feature low-fat products. However, most grocery stores are also filled with high-fat convenience foods. So watch out and don't go shopping when you're hungry!

If you need to shop at a grocery store for all or much of your food, make conscious choices to pick out the healthiest products possible and avoid the aisles or sections of the stores that have high-fat foods.

If the unhealthy food isn't in your cupboard. Then you can't eat it. (At least not immediately! Don't pick up the phone and order that Pizza!)

Only buying food that is great for you not only helps your health, but also helps to remove temptation from your path (especially at midnight when you are feeling peckish)

Tip: When shopping in a grocery store, do your shopping around the perimeter of the store. This is usually where the produce sections are. Avoid the centre aisles, where chips, pop, cookies, and other high-fat foods tend to lurk.

5) Convenience Stores

You should avoid shopping in convenience stores wherever possible. They tend to have higher prices and focus on selling high-fat and processed foods that are prominently displayed. Healthy foods are often at the back and fresh produce tends to be in less than fresh states. Since these stores are tiny and specialize in "convenience foods," there is usually very little variety of healthy options available.

If you want to lower your cholesterol over the next month, avoid shopping at convenience stores wherever possible.

6) Cafeterias, Cafes and Restaurants

Since cafeterias, cafes, and restaurants are businesses; they want to make money by having you enjoy their food enough to purchase more of it. For this reason, these places worry more about taste than about heart-health. Understandable, but not good for your priorities if you are trying to lower your cholesterol.

High-fat foods are on many restaurant and cafeteria menus, often disguised in sauces on otherwise healthy food and if you want to lower your cholesterol, you need to be vigilant about what's on the menu.

Some more food tips...

Avoid buying prepared or pre-packaged food, whether from grocery stores or restaurants.

Brown-bag your lunch and arrange to meet friends somewhere else besides a restaurant. If you need to eat at a restaurant, choose the smallest portions of the plainest foods available.

This is better than ordering the salad, assuming that it will be healthier. A salad packed with bacon bits and cheese can sometimes be among the highest-fat items on a menu!

Instead, choose dishes that seem to have low-fat elements, such as skinless chicken or fruits. Ask for dressings on the side and eat around any high-fat items such as cheese.

Avoid cream sauces.

You don't need to completely change the way you shop in order to lower your cholesterol, but stopping by the farmer's market once a week and avoiding convenience stores and restaurants will make it that much easier to find a terrific variety of fresh heart-healthy foods that you will enjoy eating.

After all, how good your diet is depends on the ingredients you put into your food.

How you shop can be as important as where you shop. Taking a few simple steps can make it easier for you to choose foods that will help you lower your cholesterol:

Four Shopping Tips

1) Shop for food once a week

Plan your menu for each week ahead of time and select one day a week for food shopping. This will minimize the amount of time you spend thinking about food and will reduce the chances that you forget items or over shop (and overeat).

2) Shop after eating

Shopping on an empty stomach will encourage impulse buying. Your willpower will also be at its weakest when you are hungry, making you more likely to reach for fatty comfortfoods.

So shop on a full stomach. Your will power will be much stronger, and the choices you make will be likely to be better.

3) Choose a time to shop when the stores are not too full and the selection is at its height

At farmer's markets and greengrocers, the selection may be best earlier in the day. You can ask your grocery store when their deliveries of produce are scheduled.

If you shop when stores are uncrowded and selection is good, you are more likely to have the time to make good choices and you will be able to enjoy a selection that makes healthy eating easy.

If budget is a priority then another good time to shop (especially at farmer's markets and greengrocers) is shortly before they are due to close. At that time you can often pick up fruit and vegetables either free (as otherwise it may spoil and they would have to throw it anyway), or at a massive discount.

At this time of the day it can pay big dividends to try to haggle for a discount.

The worst time to food shop is in the middle of the day when everyone else does their shopping. Choice is often poor because early supplies have run out and the shelves have not been re-stocked. The stores are crowded and so everything takes longer to find. And it's too early for haggling, so little chance of discounts.

4) Stick to a list

Plan your shopping list based on your weekly menu ahead of time and stick to the list to prevent overbuying and overeating.

The only exception to this should be fresh fruits and vegetables you see that may make good snacks. You can buy some of these if you find fresh produce that you have not tried before or produce that is on sale.

In general, though, buy only what you need each week so that you will have complete meals rather than food that goes bad before you get a chance to eat it.

And be sure to check the food labels on any other products you are buying so you are getting the best choice possible (See *Appendix 3 – Learn To Read Food Labels* for more detailed information)

Shopping at online supermarkets can help with this, as not only do their systems normally remember items you have previously purchased, but you can also arrange to have them deliver your shopping at a time that suits your lifestyle.

If you are in the United States you can find a big list of US Online Supermarkets here:

www.supermarketpage.com/onlinesupermarkets.php

(That same link also has a nice list of online Organic Food Suppliers)

If you are in the United Kingdom you can find a big list of UK Online Supermarkets here:

www.shopsafe.co.uk/supermarkets.asp

Simplify Your Shopping Cart!

The fact is that many of us don't have a lot of time to do food shopping. With our other responsibilities and our crammed schedules, we don't usually have the time to research our food well before we buy, and our shopping trips may feel rushed.

If that describes you, there is an easy way to make sure that your shopping cart has the foods you need to stay heart healthy:

6 Steps To Checking Your Shopping Cart

1) Have as much food in there as you think you will need until your next shop. Do not buy more or you may end up overeating.

2) Your cart should include plentiful amounts of fresh fruits and vegetables (including fresh herbs).

3) You should have less (significantly less) grains than vegetables and fruits. These should be simple (not prepared or pre-seasoned or flavoured) and whole-grain where possible. Check the labels on your breads and baked products to make sure that you are getting as little fat and sodium in these products as possible.

Favour whole grains like oats and barley over white breads. Include at least some nuts (unsalted, unflavoured, and not roasted).

Avoid bakery products like cookies and sweets entirely or buy very few (one cookie instead of a packet, and, where possible, check that it has no trans fats).

4) Check to make sure that you have significantly less meats and animal proteins than you have grains. Those meats you have should be lean where possible. Choose fish and poultry over other meats and choose the leanest cuts of meat you can.

Buy less meat than you usually would and buy it as plain as possible (avoid seasoned, precooked, prepared, or processed meats such as sausages).

5) You should have very little fats at all, and those should be healthy and have high percentages of monounsaturated fat.

Choose extra virgin olive oil and avoid hydrogenated oils, palm oils, or any oils that are high in saturated or trans fats (read the labels).

6) Try to eliminate as many packaged foods as you can. Anything that has been cooked processed and prepared for you ahead of time or contains flavourings or seasonings should be given a second hard look before finding its way into your basket.

These packages are usually brightly coloured and contain logos and brand names. These should form the smallest portion of your shopping cart.

Your cholesterol will fall even more quickly if you eliminate them entirely.

At the very least, read the labels of these products to choose the products with the lowest sodium and fat levels possible. (*See Appendix 3*)

Checking your shopping cart takes only a few minutes and following only these six simple steps will put you much further along towards lowering your cholesterol.

Here is a Quick Shopping Cheat Sheet to consider the next time you go food shopping.

This is the good cholesterol choices and the ones to be more wary of when you go shopping.

Good Food Choices

1/ Whole grain cereals, oats, and cereals that have psyllium and flaxseed.
2/ Any types of fruits.
3/ Grains such as quinoa, barley, hominy, millet, amaranth, bulgur, cous cous.
4/ Nuts (almonds, pecans, walnuts all with no additives like salt and all untoasted).
5/ Dried legumes, beans, peas, lentils.
6/ Vegetables of all kinds (fresh where possible, but frozen is ok too).
7/ Soybean products such as tofu and soy milk.
8/ Whole wheat, rye, pumpernickel bread (look for low-salt varieties and check levels of fats first).
9/ Avocado.
10/ Tortillas, whole grain pita breads and crackers (make sure to get low-salt varieties and check fat amounts).
11/ Fresh garlic and herbs, dried spices and herbs.
12/ Low-sodium salsa or spicy sauce.
13/ Low fat and low sodium soup base or stock.
14/ Low sodium pasta sauce.
15/ Lean meats and skinless chicken.
16/ Fish.

17/ Olive Oil.
18/ Low fat dairy products and egg whites.
19/ Rice and pastas.
20/ Popcorn that can be air-popped.
21/ Water.
22/ Freshly squeezed fruit juice.

Be Careful Of...

1/ Whole eggs and Whole milk products
2/ Red meat that is fatty (looks marbleized)
3/ Organ meats
4/ Processed or prepared foods (heat and serve foods or sandwich meats and sausages)
5/ Granola or Muesli cereals (many contain lots of fats)
6/ Sports drinks, sodas, fruit "beverages" (many are high in salts as well as sugars)

Also, watch out for these ingredients or food values on food labels (Less is better)

1/ Sodium
2/ Salt
3/ Shortening (fat or lard from an animal or vegetable)
4/ Hydrogenated or partially hydrogenated oil
5/ Fats (especially trans fats and saturated fats)

Chapter 8
Ten Cholesterol Goldmine Resources, One Must Have Item and The Cholesterol Revitaliser Power Summary

There are a number of places you will want to check in order to find more help with lowering your cholesterol. Consider the following resources:

Ten Cholesterol Goldmine Resources

1) Your library

Your library will have many resources that can help you with lowering your cholesterol. From library books about cholesterol to cookbooks that feature heart-friendly recipes, the library should be one of your first stops when you are looking for resources.

In addition to books on the subject that you can read immediately. You can also order others at no charge from the library catalogue, and have access to specific information about local health facilities available in your community.

2) Your local hospital or clinic

Whether it is research studies that allow you to try new treatments to lower your cholesterol, pamphlets about cholesterol, or experts that can answer all your questions, clinics and hospitals are a great place to find the information you need to stay healthy. A quick search online will find your local ones.
Give them a call and see if they run any cholesterol clinics.

3) Professional groups

You can contact the *National Center for Nutrition and Dietetics of the American Dietetic Association* if you need a registered dietician to help you in choosing the right foods.

www.eatright.org

You can also contact groups such as the *American Heart Association*.

www.americanheart.org

The *Canadian Heart and Stroke Association*

www.heartandstroke.ca

In the UK you should check :

www.heartuk.org.uk

These organizations also host fund-raising efforts to help raise awareness of heart issues and to raise funds for research. This can be a great way to get involved in helping to improve the lives of everyone affected by high cholesterol levels.

In the UK you can also get advice and immediate assistance for any health problem directly from the UK Governments NHS Direct website

www.nhsdirect.nhs.uk or call 0845 4647

4) Online support groups

These groups are invaluable for giving you tips, recipes, and support that can make lowering your cholesterol easier to achieve.

The American Heart Association for example (**www.americanheart.org**) has a forum section specifically dedicated to Cholesterol Management.

And you can also check out (**www.health.gov**) which is a health portal website that the United States Government provides to all manner of interesting health resources. It can seem a little confusing in all honesty. But the breadth of information that is available if you dig a little is amazing.

5) In-person support groups

These often meet at libraries or other public places and can be a good way to get support and find out how others deal with high cholesterol and cholesterol-lowering treatments and medications.

Your local health clinic or Doctor may also be able to provide information about suitable local groups.

6) Computer programs

There are many different computer programs and planners you can buy that can prompt you to take your medication, allow you to create a computer cholesterol log, and keep track of your daily calories, fat grams, sodium intake, and cholesterol.

Go to **www.downloads.com** and do a search for 'cholesterol' and you will see a large choice of the latest programs that you can use. Some of them cost money. But most offer free thirty day trials, and many are free.

If you have an iPhone then be sure to visit the Apple App Store and do a search for health apps that you can download.

www.apple.com/iphone/apps-for-iphone/

It is by no means necessary to do this. Keeping track by hand works fine as well, but if you really want to keep track of your health on your computer (or phone), then at least you now know that it is possible.

7) Food guides

These handy guides are sold at many bookstores and can tell you exactly how much cholesterol, sodium, fat, and other elements are contained in the food you eat.

You can also check out **www.amazon.com** that has a specific section dedicated to '*Food Counters*' in their Diets and Weight Loss books section. (It is in the "Health, Mind and Body" Books Section)

I.e. Books > Health, Mind and Body > Diets & Weight Loss > Food Counters

(Here is a shortened link - **http://bit.ly/6W6yB1**)

A good tip here is to nip along to your local weight loss club night. Not because you necessarily need to diet, but because these folks will be bang up to date on the pros and cons of these books. And will likely be able to recommend which one is currently the best.

(There are over 800 listed on Amazon as of this writing! But because dieters often rely on them so heavily, they are a constantly updating source of which is the latest and greatest)

If in doubt just pop along to your local bookstore and browse through a selection.

Try looking for a few identical foodstuffs in several different guides, and see which ones come up with the best, most useable information.

Amazon.com also has a useful feature called '*Search Inside*' so you can actually take a look at the layout of a book before buying.

This is incredibly useful for this type of book. Because to be frank about it, some of them are just plain confusing!

So compare a few before spending your cash.

8) Medical supplies

There are counters and monitors that can help you to keep track of your blood pressure and cholesterol at home. These can be handy in the long run for keeping track of your progress. If you do a search on Google for '*cholesterol monitors*' then you will be inundated with choice. Though be aware that some can be quite expensive. ($100 -$500)

There are also cheaper 'once only' type testing kits that are around the $25 to $35 range that will also come up when you do that search.

These can be useful if you live in a particularly remote location and have difficulty getting to a doctor or clinic to get measured regularly.

But please note. You should be consulting with your Doctor about your cholesterol lowering regime anyway, so you will need to make arrangements to make sure that he is kept up to date. That being the case you could just get it measured at your doctor's surgery.

9) Cholesterol clinics

As cholesterol becomes a bigger issue, many pharmacies, hospitals, and clinics offer free workshops, free information sessions, and even free cholesterol testing.
If you are in the United States then check out this resource:

http://ask.hrsa.gov/pc/

It is a US wide searchable database of *Health Centers* ("centres" in the UK) that are available even if you have no health insurance.

In the UK you can find a Searchable database of *Lipid Clinics* (which deal with people at cardiovascular risk, including high cholesterol) here:

www.heartuk.org.uk/lipidclinics/index.php

Elsewhere consult with your Doctor who will also be able to point you in the right direction for other help that is available.

10) Pharmacies

Many pharmacists have a vast knowledge of cholesterol and heart medications, conditions, and treatments. Many pharmacies have pamphlets, booklets, and even videos that can inform you about treatments and options. Your local pharmacy can be a great place to learn more about keeping your heart safe.

The Must Have Item... Medical Alert Bracelets

These bracelets tell health care professionals if you have heightened cholesterol, other serious conditions, or are on cholesterol medication.

If you are injured or unable to speak for yourself in a medical emergency, these bracelets can tell health care professionals which treatments can help you and which can harm you.

If you have been told you have elevated cholesterol, you may consider getting one of these inexpensive bracelets at your local pharmacy.

Cholesterol Revitaliser Power Summary

By now, you understand what cholesterol is and what you need to do to keep your cholesterol level healthy and your heart in good condition.

There is a lot of information in Cholesterol Revitaliser, and that is why you will want to take the time to look over it again to refresh your memory and to get more ideas for lowering your cholesterol.

Even though the tips and information in Cholesterol Revitaliser will help lower your cholesterol quickly (if you apply it), this book is about a lot more than just a month or two in your life.

Lower cholesterol is a life-long commitment to better health. You need to keep working on good health to keep your cholesterol levels and your body fighting fit.

The ideas in this book aren't just to help you get your cholesterol back to acceptable levels so that you can return to your old eating habits. The ideas are designed to help you make permanent changes in your life that can help keep you healthy for life.

Throughout you have been encouraged to ask questions of yourself and take actions that can help to improve your health. If you are not sure where to start or are feeling overwhelmed at this point, consider this fast checklist of getting started to lowering your cholesterol.

Ok. Start doing these things today:

30 Power Summary Tips to Refresh Your Memory About What We Have Covered

1/ See a doctor to have your cholesterol levels checked and to get personalized advice about keeping healthy.

2/ Eat more fresh fruit fruits and vegetables. Make sure you get plenty of variety of these.

3/ Eat fish, leaner cuts of meat and poultry.

4/ Use low-fat dairy products (Or go Vegetarian)

5/ Cut back on salt and fats in your cooking.

6/ Add flavour with herbs and spices and garlic. You can also add flavour by marinating foods in lemon juice, spices, or pureed fruits or vegetables.

7/ Broil, bake, grill, steam, or poach your food rather than frying.

8/ If you smoke, stop.

9/ Exercise for thirty minutes at least every other day. But preferably every day.

10/ Get your body to a healthy body weight. Ask your doctor what this should be for you.

11/ Check food labels. Buy foods that are low in fats, and have few saturated, preferably no trans-fats, and are higher in Mono-Unsaturated and Poly-Unsaturated fats.

12/ Eat at home more often, rather than eating at restaurants or getting take out.

13/ Learn to prepare your own low-fat and heart-healthy meals that you enjoy.

14/ If you do eat out, choose the leanest foods you can. Ask for dressings and sauces on the side or ask them to be left out entirely.

15/ Eat smaller portions of foods, but eat more regularly to keep your blood sugar more stable.

16/ Try adding more avocados into your diet.

17/ Follow your doctor's directions about cholesterol treatment as precisely as you can.

18/ Cut out coffee for the next month or at least try to cut down if you are drinking a lot of coffee.

19/ Learn all you can about cholesterol and healthy eating so that you can make better choices.

20/ Visit some of the Cholesterol Health and information sites I have listed throughout the book.

21/ Visit a Farmers Market or Health Food Shop in the next few weeks.

22/ Swap butter in your diet for the cholesterol lowering plant sterol brands such as Benecol.

23/ Make healthy eating more convenient by having low-fat and heart-healthy snacks and meals readily available in your home.

24/ Replace existing snack choices with healthy new ones (And learn to love them!)

25/ Get rid of high-fat and unhealthy foods in your home and replace them with tasty but healthy foods that are good for you.

26/ Keep a cholesterol journal that details your foods, your exercise, your cholesterol treatment, your symptoms, your questions, and your progress. Update it daily to have an accurate reflection of your actions.

27/ Stay Positive and learn to relax. Taking up something like meditation can help you feel calmer.

28/ Start a media diet and spend your time doing something more active instead of watching television for hours on end.

29/ Get a juicer and start making your own delicious smoothies and shakes.

30/ Take another read through Chapter 4 on 'Cholesterol Treatments' and consider trying some of the many different cholesterol lowering herbal and medical alternatives). For example Pantethine and Niacin (after having checked first with your Doctor)

These tips are a good place to start as you quickly start implementing the many ideas in Cholesterol Revitaliser that can help you lower your cholesterol.

Be assured. You can get great results on your road to a healthier revitalised you and onwards to an entire lifetime of lower cholesterol and feeling great.

Remember to read this book again and review it regularly so that you don't miss any information that you may have glossed over on a first reading.

Start taking the steps you need TODAY to get your cholesterol under control!

Take Care and Take Action!

Stuart Brown

P.S If you have enjoyed this book then please write a positive review on Amazon so that others can get to benefit as well.

You can find this book at the following web addresses on Amazon:

US - www.amazon.com/dp/0956436307
UK - www.amazon.co.uk/dp/0956436307
Canada - www.amazon.ca/dp/0956436307

Thanks.

Appendix 1
The Amazing Choice of Vegetables

Ok. Here are some vegetables you could, and should be eating:

Remember, as Helen Keller said:

'Life is either a daring adventure or nothing at all'.

So eat as though you believe it! Be daring.

- Anise
- Alfalfa sprouts
- Artichoke
- Arugula
- Asparagus
- Bean Varieties (there are many different kinds of beans, from black beans, borlotti beans, broad beans, chickpeas, green beans, kidney beans, runner beans, soy beans, red beans, mung beans, navy beans, lima beans to azuki beans, and many others)
- Bean sprouts
- Lentils
- Peas (again, there are many delicious brands of peas, many which you likely have not tried before. These may include snow peas, green peas, sugar snap peas, and many others)
- Beets and beet greens
- Bok choy
- Breadfruit
- Broccoli
- Brussels sprouts

- Cabbage (there are many kinds, ranging from red and green to Chinese cabbage and others)
- Calabrese
- Carrots
- Cauliflower
- Celery
- Chard
- Chicory
- Collard
- Corn
- Celeriac
- Daikon
- Eggplant
- Endive
- Fennel (whole fennel, not just the seeds, can be used in cooking)
- Fiddleheads
- Frisee
- Garlic
- Chives
- Kai-lan
- Kale
- Kohlrabi
- Leek
- Lemon grass
- Onions
- Lettuce (if you have always eaten iceberg lettuce, you will be stunned by the range of lettuces out there, including Bibb and many others)
- Mushrooms (There are many types of mushrooms, from the common to the exotic, and they can easily be bought fresh or dried to add flavour to just about every meal)
- Mustard greens

- Nettles
- Okra
- Pepper Varieties (from hot peppers like the habanero and others to sweet green, orange, yellow and red peppers, these vegetables are very good for you and extremely tasty)
- Spinach
- Radicchio
- Rapini
- Parsnips
- Radishes
- Rutabaga
- Turnip and turnip greens
- Skirret
- Squashes (there are many of these, from butternut to acorn to pumpkins and gourds. Also be sure to try gem squash and spaghetti squash)
- Zucchini
- Cucumber
- Tomatoes (these range from hot house tomatoes to cherry and grape tomatoes -their taste, not just their size, differs)
- Tubers
- Potatoes (from yams and sweet potatoes to new potatoes, red potatoes, and others, these vegetables present an almost infinite variety)
- Water chestnuts
- Watercress

Remember to keep trying new vegetables every week!

Appendix 2
Getting Fruity

Consider the following list of all the fresh fruits you may not have tried yet.

It is a reminder of all the delicious fruits you could be eating.

Albert Einstein, the esteemed physicist, once said:

"A table, a chair, a bowl of fruit and a violin. What else does a man need to be happy?"

So, think about that the next time you are out shopping and considering drifting on by the fruit section to get to the cookies!

If a bowl of fruit is good enough for Mr Genius, then it is good enough for you and I ☺

Here are some to try

• Apples (there are an almost infinite variety of apples, some quite rare. Try the following varieties:

Akane, Arlet, Blushing Golden, Braeburn, Centennial Crab, Chieftain, Cortland, Empire, Empress, Fuji, Gala, Honey Crisp, Jonagold, Kandil Sinap, Liberty, Mantet, Mcintosh, Mutsu, Northern Spy, Patricia, Red Astrachan, Red Secor, Russet, Starr, Virginia Gold, Yataka, Yellow Transparent, Wilson Juicy, and the many others available at your grocery store and farmer's market)

    • Apricots
    • Avocado
    • Bananas (try Fruit Bananas, Apple Bananas, Baby Bananas, Baking Bananas, Red bananas, and others)

- Berries (besides the usual strawberries and raspberries, there are dewberries, boysenberries, loganberries, cloudberries, wineberries, bearberries, bilberries, blueberries, cranberries, huckleberries, lingonberries, barberries, currants, elderberries, gooseberries, nannyberries, sea grapes, crowberries, and others)
- Cherries (from sour cherries, Monmorency cherries, and sweet cherries such as Black Russians, Chinooks, Lapins, Hedelfingers, and others)
- Clementines
- Dates
- Figs
- Grapefruits
- Grapes (there are many, many kinds, ranging from pale greens to very deep purples)
- Guava
- Kiwis
- Kumquats
- Lemons and Limes
- Lychee fruits
- Mangos
- Melons (Red water, Canary, Canteloupe, Cassava, Honeydew, Watermelon, and others)
- Nectarines
- Oranges
- Papayas
- Passion Fruits
- Peaches (including Encore, Reliance, Red Haven, and Sensation Dwarf Peach, among others)
- Pears (including Asian pears, Beirschmidt, Bartlett, and others)
- Persimmons
- Pineapples

- Plums (including Mt. Royal Plum, Opal, Stanley Prune Plum, Unize Plum, Dietz, Empress Prune Plum, Starking Delicious Plum, and many others)
- Pomegranates
- Pummelo
- Rhubarb
- Star Fruit

And that is just a small selection!

Keep experimenting.

Appendix 3
Learn to Read Food Labels

Food labels are something you will have to pay attention to when you go shopping. Manufacturers of foods in North America and Europe are required to provide accurate information about their food products. You can find this information on food labels, and most food labels today are made to be easy-to-read.

There are several elements to a food label:

• *Identification*

The front of the food label or package will tell you the brand of the product and what the product is.

• *Information about the manufacturer*

Most food packages will tell you where a food was made, who imported it (if the food was imported) and how you can contact the manufacturer or importer. This information can be useful if you want to contact someone about the exact food value content of a product or if you have a question or complaint about the food.

• *Codes and expiry dates*

Most food packages contain codes and numbers that contain information about where the product was made and when. Often, expiry dates are listed somewhere among these numbers. It is a good habit to glance at expiry dates of your food to make sure that you are getting the freshest product available.

Supermarkets tend to make it a practice to put the freshest products at the back of the shelves, because they want to sell the older stock first. So make sure that you root around at the back of the shelf and compare the expiry dates of the same products.

• *Logos, advertisements, and claims*

Many foods will have logos or claims on the front of the label or food packaging. These may contain terms such as *"light"*, *"the best"*, *"healthy"*, *"natural"* and others.

These will likely catch your attention when you are looking for heart-healthy choices. However, you should never take this information at face value. Treat these claims as advertisements rather than as facts.

Many foods that claim to be "low fat" often simply have smaller portion sizes.

So still check carefully

• *Ingredients*

This is where the information starts to get really useful. Almost all packaged products have lists of ingredients used in the making of the product. To know how healthy a food really is, you should start here. Ingredients are listed in order of amount. That means that if a label reads *"peanut butter, sugar, chocolate solids"*, the product contains mostly peanut butter, with less sugar than peanut butter, and less chocolate solids than sugar.

(Ingredients listed in brackets are ingredients that are part of something else or contain more information about an ingredient.)

For example, if an ingredients list reads "*Vitamins –* *(thiamin hydrochloride, niacin amide, folic acid)*", then the vitamins in the food consist of thiamin hydrochloride, niacin amide and folic acid.

When shopping to lower your cholesterol, or just to check you are eating healthily, always read the ingredients list.

Look for foods that contain healthy foods first on the in-gredient list (meaning that there are more of these foods) and foods that have ingredient lists that contain few saturated fats.

• *Low cholesterol*

Foods that are lower in dietary cholesterol are obviously great for our purposes, and some products will actually make a sell-ing point of this. So look out for those.

• *Percentages*

The right hand side of many labels will tell you what percentage of the "*recommended daily value*" the food represents.

For example, a product may claim to provide 30% of a day's recommended daily amount of iron. This means that one serving size of the food will give 30% of the iron you need all day.

• *Nutrition facts*

This is where you need to turn your eyes every time you pick up a food you may want to eat. Even if you can't understand half the ingredients on the ingredients list, even if you are not sure what you are looking for, this is the section of the food label that can help you separate claims from facts.

Food labels in North America now contain a simplified section of information about the food. This is often found on the side of the box or the back of a food package.

This part of the label lists portion sizes, the per cent or amount of fats, vitamins and other nutrients the food provides, and the amounts of fats and calories the food contains.

This is information you can use. Each time that you pick up a food item, look at the label. Check the portion size, the amount of fats and the types of fats in the food. (For fruit and vegetables a good pocket sized '*Calorie Guide*' will give you the same information)

The amount of saturated and trans fats should be very small and the portion size should be large.

For example, consider a serving of cream. For a 15 ml serving (one tablespoon) the cream has 1 gram of saturated fats. While the amount of fat is small, the serving is small too, meaning that the product is actually 8% fat.

Soy milk, a much better alternative, has 1 gram of saturated fat in a two cup serving, making it much lower in saturated fat.

When making healthy choices, check this part of every food label for the following:

• *Serving Size*

This will tell you whether a food is really healthy or whether it just appears so due to a very tiny portion size (remember my tic-tac example...)

• *Fat Levels*

Look at the gram amounts of trans and saturated fats. The lower the better.

• *Sodium*

Look for foods that contain as little salt as possible.

• *Calories*

Choosing lower-calorie foods is generally better for your heart, your cholesterol level, and your overall health. (Though fruits such as avocado can be an exception)

• *Fibre*

Foods high in fibre ('fiber' in the US) are good for your health and cholesterol level.

When shopping for foods, make sure to choose foods that have the lowest percentages for values such as sodium, cholesterol, and fats, and higher percentages for values such as fibre. This will help ensure that you are making heart-healthy choices.

You may notice that a number of foods do not contain food labels at all. Foods sold in bulk, fresh produce, home-made foods (foods sold at bake sales or at farmer's stands) and prepared foods in restaurants and cafeterias do not have these labels.

In the case of fresh produce and some bulk foods (dried legumes, lentils, and spices) this doesn't always matter, as you generally know that these foods are healthy.

On the other hand, no food labels are a good reason to avoid restaurant and take-out meals, as you have no control or choice over how much food you are eating.

Often, you can just tap into your own common sense. If you are being honest, you KNOW that lettuce is healthier than Pizza! ☺

Some restaurants have begun to offer ingredient lists and food value information about their meals, but this information is not always easy to find, though it is sometimes posted in the kitchen or on the restaurants web page.

In the future, it is possible that more restaurants will offer patrons this information so that diners can make more informed decisions about what to eat.

The more people start demanding this information, the sooner it will be provided as standard with the menu.

So the next time you eat out ask for it, and see what they say. The "worst" that can happen is that they won't have any information. And at the very least if a few people start asking for nutritional information it gives the restaurant a business incentive to provide it.

What many people don't realize is that fast food restaurants like McDonalds already have detailed nutritional information available on their websites about the foods they serve. (And in their restaurants, though they are not usually easy to find) And others like Burger King and KFC also do.

So if you dig around you can become more informed about the foods that you are eating in restaurants and fast food establishments.

But, in general, you are better off buying and cooking your own food. Because that way you will know **exactly** what you are eating.

A good tip here if you really want to know the nutritional content of the food you are eating is to invest in a food guide. This will allow you to estimate how much salt, fat and calories there is in what you are eating.

You could even take such a guide into restaurants and the supermarket with you, as they are generally pocket sized for portability.

These are readily available in bookshops or online and are very cheap, so it's well worth getting one.

It makes sense and is quite eye opening to know what you are putting in your body with the foods you are eating.

And also because eating the right kind of fats is so crucial to lowering your cholesterol.

Glossary
The 18 Cholesterol Terms
You MUST Understand

As you lower your cholesterol, you will encounter new words and terms.

Here are 18 key terms. As you get used to these new concepts, feel free to turn to this glossary to help you recall what they mean:

Atherosclerosis
If you have too much cholesterol in the blood, it will create a yellow thick substance on the lining of the blood vessels. This is known as atherosclerosis. If it continues to grow, it can block blood vessels, leading to a stroke or heart attack. This is a key risk of having high bad (LDL) cholesterol levels.

Blood Cholesterol
Blood cholesterol is wax-like material that is made by the body. Blood cholesterol is needed to keep cells healthy, to create hormones, and to keep the body functioning. Too much, though, increases your risk of atherosclerosis.

Dietary Cholesterol
Dietary cholesterol is the cholesterol found in some of your food. Since all animals produce cholesterol, dietary cholesterol is found in the foods that are made from animals (foods such as meat, dairy products, fish, and eggs). To stay heart-healthy, you will want to avoid eating too much dietary cholesterol.

Cholesterol Profile
Your cholesterol profile is a listing of your cholesterol levels. This includes your LDL, HDL, your total cholesterol, and tri-

glycerides. Your doctor finds this information through a blood test. Your cholesterol profile helps medical professionals determine how at risk you are from developing certain complications associated with high cholesterol levels.

Essential Fatty Acids

Your body needs fats to survive, and especially to build cells. The fats your body needs to get from the foods you eat are called essential fatty acids. The two 'families' of essential fatty acids are Omega 3 and Omega 6, and getting fats from both these in the diet is essential as they cannot be made by the body. Fish and Hemp Seeds are good sources.

Fibre (Or 'Fiber' in the US)

Fibre is the part of plants that cannot be digested by us. There are two types of fibre: insoluble and soluble. Both are important to health. Insoluble fibre in grains and fruits and vegetables is what keeps you "regular" and keeps your bowels in good shape. The soluble fibre found in oats, barley, and other plants has been found to lower cholesterol levels. If you are trying to lower your cholesterol and stay healthy, eating a diet with adequate fibre can help.

High Density Lipoproteins (HDL)

This is known as the "good" cholesterol, and is generated by the liver. HDL transports cholesterol and fats to your liver from your arteries. In the liver, the fats can be broken down or recycled for your body to use. If you have high levels of HDL, chances are your heart is healthy, since the cholesterol is being effectively transported rather than being left in your blood, where it can cause a hardening of the arteries. If your levels of HDL are low, you may be putting your heart at risk.

Hydrogenated Fats

These are fats you want to avoid in your diet if you want to lower bad cholesterol levels. Hydrogenated fats are fats either polyunsaturated or monounsaturated that have been treated with hydrogen atoms to guarantee a longer shelf life. The process of hydrogenation causes fats to become saturated fats.

Lipid Specialists

These doctors specialize in the treatment of treating high blood cholesterol and related health issues. If you have very high cholesterol and traditional methods of lowering your cholesterol and risk for heart disease do not work, you may be referred to a lipid specialist for specialized treatment.

Low Density Lipoproteins (LDL)

Also called "bad cholesterol", LDL are manufactured by the liver. Its job it to transport fats, including cholesterol, from the liver to the areas of your body that need the fats (such as your organs, muscles, and your tissues). If your LDL levels are high, it suggests that there is plenty of cholesterol in your blood, which increases the chances of clogged arteries, which is in turn very dangerous for your heart.

Monounsaturated Fats

These fats are liquids at room temperature. These fats are also good for you because when eaten in place of carbohydrates they can raise your HDL (good cholesterol) levels and lower your LDL (bad cholesterol levels). Look for products that have these fats if you want to stay heart-healthy. Monounsaturated fats are found in high concentrations in olive oil, canola oil and peanuts.

Omega 6

This is actually a "family" of fatty acids that increase your good cholesterol level while lowering your bad cholesterol. This makes Omega-6 a great food source for staying healthy. You can find these fatty acids in nuts, grains, vegetables, and vegetable oils. They are part of the reason why you are encouraged to eat these foods in your low-cholesterol diet.

Polyunsaturated Fats

These fats are liquid at room temperature. They are a better choice than saturated fats. In small amounts, these fats may lower bad cholesterol. Polyunsaturated fats are found in high concentrations in soybean oils, corn and sunflower oils.

Processed Foods

Processed foods are foods that have been treated before being sold. In some cases, processed foods are treated to eliminate bacteria or make foods healthier. For example, the process of pasteurization eliminates some of the harmful elements in milk that can make us sick.

Most of our foods are processed in some way. However, some foods are processed in order to change their taste or in order to give them a longer shelf-life. The processing that it takes to do this sometimes involves adding fats, salts and other unhealthy ingredients or involves heating the foods until some or much of the nutrient value is lost.

When choosing processed foods, it is important to choose foods that have as few detrimental ingredients as possible. In general, foods that have had more done to them (such as deli meats, potato chips and cookies) and foods that are considered "fast foods" or convenience foods (such as hamburgers, prepared hors d'oeuvres, and cocktail snacks, among others) are higher in fats and salt.

Read the labels of all processed foods to understand exactly what you are eating and how these foods may affect your health.

Saturated Fats

These fats are solid at room temperature. They are also likely to raise your bad cholesterol. If you want to lower your cholesterol, avoid, or at least cut down your intake of these fats in your food. In many cases, saturated fats come from animal proteins and products (meats, and milk products). They are also found in hydrogenated vegetable oil and in coconut and palm oil.

Trans Fatty Acids

These are another fat group you will want to avoid. They are hydrogenated and increase bad cholesterol while lowering good cholesterol. They are actually **far worse** than even saturated fats in terms of raising your cholesterol levels and increasing your risk of heart disease. Bottom line. Avoid eating trans-fat wherever possible.

Triglycerides

Triglycerides are a fat, like cholesterol, which is transported in the blood stream. This fat is the culprit behind most of the fat in the body. Like LDL Cholesterol, it can form a thick goo and block arteries if there is too much of it in the blood. As you lower your bad cholesterol, you will also want to keep your triglycerides low. Often, high triglycerides are caused by drinking too much alcohol, overeating (or being overweight) and not enough physical exercise.

Very Low Density Lipoproteins (VLDL)

These lipoproteins transport cholesterol from the liver to the body's organs and tissues that need it. Studies have shown that high levels of these lipoproteins may be a risk factor for heart disease. Not all cholesterol profiles include a number for VLDLs, but if yours does, work to keep the levels low.

Index

low density lipoproteins, 22,
175, 178
low fat, 20, 29, 35, 36, 44, 46,
51, 52, 53, 54, 55, 64, 77, 78,
80, 93, 100, 103, 112, 122,
123, 124, 129, 135, 136, 138,
152, 153, 154, 166
low fat cooking sprays, 29
low fat diet, 35, 36
low-salt broth, 44
low-sodium, 53, 54
lung cancer, 90

M

make good food more
appealing, 119
margarines, 39, 41, 43, 76, 104
Martha Kubik, 112
mashed avocado, 52
maximum daily intake of meat,
45
McDonalds, 29, 114, 115, 170
medical alert bracelets, 151
medication, 25, 28, 61, 62, 70,
72, 74, 75, 92, 97, 98, 102,
147, 151
medications, 16, 21, 57, 69, 71,
72, 73, 74, 92, 98, 99, 100,
103, 147, 150
men, 25, 30, 36, 65, 82, 86, 87,
90, 91, 104
menopause, 67, 73, 102, 104,
105
meta analyses, 64
meta-analysis, 79
metabolic rate, 78
Mevacor, 71
Microwaving, 44

milk, 40, 53, 56, 80, 93, 126,
143, 144, 168, 176, 177
milligrams per deciliter of
blood, 23, 24, 25, 26, 27, 36,
37, 59, 63, 64, 79, 87, 90, 105,
126
moderate intensity exercise, 82
monounsaturated fat, 40, 41,
42, 77, 78, 142, 175
Morgan Spurlock, 29
muscle problems, 72
muscular endurance, 87

N

National Center for Health
Statistics, 32
National Center for Nutrition,
146
natural health practioner, 68
natural therapies, 62
Naturopath, 57
nausea, 61, 72, 87
nematode worm study, 38
New York Stop Smoking
Medical Center, 91
NHS Direct, 146
niacin, 20, 59, 61, 62, 63, 155,
167
Nicotine, 91
Nicotinic acid, 61
normal, 22, 24, 25, 27, 29, 48,
59, 119
nutrition, 28, 33, 51, 60, 61, 70,
97, 131, 167
nutritionist, 30, 39, 112, 113
nuts, 44, 52, 78, 103, 141, 143,
176

O

oats, 79, 141, 143, 174
Oats and Barley, 79
obesity, 46, 58, 74, 83, 98, 102, 104
Oklahoma University, 66
olive oil, 30, 51, 52, 68, 80, 104, 132, 142, 144, 175
omega fatty acids, 65, 80, 174, 176
online supermarkets, 140, 141
Organ meats, 43, 144
organic farms, 135
organic food suppliers, 140
osteoporosis, 67, 83

P

paediatrician, 112
pantethine, 20, 59, 60, 61, 155
pantothenic acid, 60
parchment paper, 123, 124
parenting, 111, 113
partially hydrogenated vegetable oil, 41
pasta, 54, 143
peanut oil, 40
pectin, 79
peppercorns, 88
percentage of overweight americans, 112
percentages, 20, 35, 36, 37, 42, 45, 63, 64, 65, 67, 77, 87, 90, 91, 168
pharmacies, 99, 150, 151
pick your own farms, 135
pitas, 53
placebo, 59, 62, 64

plan your meals, 126
plant phytosterol, 77
plant sterols, 20, 76, 77, 78, 104, 154
poaching, 44
Policosanol, 59
polyunsaturated fat, 40, 41, 42, 78, 80, 175, 176
postmenopausal women, 73
potassium, 78
Pravachol, 71
Pravastatin, 71
pregnant women, 65
premenopausal women, 30, 104
processed foods, 37, 43, 101, 103, 116, 137, 176
Professor Richard Weindruch, 38
psyllium, 66, 143

R

raspberry vinegar, 88
recipes, 51, 52, 54, 80, 109, 125, 130, 145, 147
recommendations for adults with regards to exercise, 82
red meat, 40, 43, 56
research studies, 20, 27, 35, 38, 46, 47, 57, 58, 59, 60, 61, 62, 63, 64, 66, 67, 68, 75, 76, 77, 78, 80, 83, 87, 88, 90, 91, 92, 93, 96, 97, 98, 112, 118, 126, 141, 145, 146
restaurants, 51, 110, 119, 120, 123, 124, 126, 127, 132, 137, 138, 153, 169, 170, 171
Rhesus Macaque Monkeys Study, 38

roasting, 44
rye, 43, 143

S

safflower, 41
salads, 39, 51, 52, 53, 76, 115, 129, 131, 138
salami, 43
salsa, 52, 53, 143
salt, 37, 38, 43, 51, 52, 53, 54, 56, 64, 75, 88, 89, 93, 121, 129, 143, 144, 152, 169, 170, 176
sandwiches, 53, 64
saturated fat, 19, 36, 39, 40, 42, 44, 45, 56, 70, 75, 101, 103, 104, 142, 144, 153, 167, 168, 175, 176, 177
sauces, 39, 54, 56, 132, 137, 138, 153
sausages, 43, 142, 144
school lunch program, 111
Selektine, 71
self-esteem, 87
sense of control, 87
shop after eating, 139
shop for food once a week, 138
shopping cart, 141
shortening, 43, 144
side effects, 58, 59, 61, 62, 63, 69, 70, 71, 72, 73, 97, 99, 103
Simvastatin, 66, 71
skimmed milk, 80
smoking, 23, 24, 26, 28, 74, 89, 90, 91, 93, 102, 104, 113
smoking facts, 90
smoothies, 54, 154

sodium, 37, 56, 88, 124, 130, 141, 142, 143, 147, 148, 169
soluble fibre, 43, 45, 66, 79, 80, 174
soy protein, 67, 76, 78, 80, 143, 157
soybean, 41, 176
soybeans, 41, 65, 143, 176
sprouts, 47, 109, 157
statins, 16, 58, 62, 66, 71, 72, 76
statistics of the amount of ads on tv, 117
Staying positive, 94
Steaming, 44
stick to a shopping list, 140
stir-frying, 44
stomach upset, 71
strawberries, 120, 162
strokes, 19, 22, 26, 32, 45, 46, 83, 90, 105, 173
sugar, 51, 56, 59, 89, 111, 144, 157, 166
sugar cane wax, 59
sunflower, 66, 176
supermarkets, 140, 141, 166
symptoms, 71, 72, 73, 95, 97, 99, 106, 154

T

Take Control, 76
Technical University, 62
testosterone, 19
The Journal of the American Medical Association, 58, 59
The National Heart, Lung and Blood Institute Family Heart Study, 46
thromboembolic stroke, 83

Lightning Source UK Ltd.
Milton Keynes UK
12 July 2010

156899UK00009B/155/P